Disclaimer

This book puts YOU in control. That is an excellent thing, but it also makes YOU responsible for using it properly. Few washing machine manufacturers will honour their guarantee if you don't follow their 'instructions for use'. In the same way, we are unable to accept liability for any loss arising from mistakes or misunderstandings on your part. So please take time to read this book carefully.

This book is not a definitive statement of the law, although we believe it to be accurate and up-to-date as of 1 September 2001. We cannot except liability for changes in the law that take place after the publication date, although every effort will be made to show any such changes on the website.

Contents

Welcome   v

Introduction   1

Buzzwords   7

Frequently asked questions   16

Spotting a doubtful customer   21

Where do I start?   24

Making it stick – enforcement   47

Sample letters and forms   92

Official forms   128

Useful contacts   171

Index   176

About the authors

Mark Fairweather is a practising solicitor, and is one of the founding partners of the legal firm Fairweather Stephenson & Co. He is co-author with Rosy Border of the Stationery Office's Simply Legal series of DIY law kits as well as several titles in the You Need This Book First series. He has two children and lives in Suffolk.

Rosy Border has worked in publishing, lecturing, journalism and the law. She is a prolific author and adapter who stopped counting after 150 titles. Rosy and her husband, John Rabson, live in Suffolk and have a married son in Tennessee.

Welcome

Welcome to the *You need This Book First* series. Let's face it – the law is a maze. You cannot hope to find your way through it without a map. This book is your map through the part of the maze that deals with getting your debtors to pay up. It contains everything lawyers would tell you about the subject, if only they had time (and you had the money to pay them).

Acknowledgements

A glance at the *Useful contacts* section will show how many individuals and organisations we consulted while compiling this book. Thank you, everyone. We would also like to thank Johnathon Rands and Fred Ford of Gotelee and Goldsmith Solicitors, who read the typescript and made some useful suggestions; and John Rabson, Chartered Engineer, for his IT support, research and refreshments.

Introduction

What this book can do for you

This book contains:

- advice on avoiding debt problems in the first place;

- advice on the steps to take before starting legal action;

- advice on the legal options;

- advice on the methods of enforcement – that is, actually getting the money after a court has ruled in your favour;

- sample letters requesting payment;

- the paperwork you need for a debt claim in the County Court;

- the paperwork you need to enforce a judgment debt;

- the paperwork you need to bankrupt an individual;

- the paperwork you need to put a company into liquidation;

- the Buzzwords which are important in this section of the law and what they mean;

- answers to some of the most frequently asked questions on the subject.

What this book can't do for you

- Be a textbook. Its job is to help you to collect your debts, not to teach you the ins and outs of contract law and court procedure. We aim to be streetwise rather than academic.

- Guarantee you will get your money.

- Replace specific advice you may need on your individual case. For example, we do not cover defended claims.

- Work outside England and Wales – the law and court procedures are different even in Scotland and Northern Ireland.

This book empowers you. Think of yourself as a driver using a road map. The map tells you the route, but it is up to you to drive carefully.

So read this book with care. Take the time to do so – do not skip anything.

- Everything is there for a purpose.
- If anything were unimportant, we would have left it out.

We have left wide margins for you to make notes.

Hazard signs

As with any legal matter, your own common sense will often tell you when you are on unfamiliar territory and need expert help. But we also alert you to common traps for the unwary. Some situations may arise which are outside the scope of this book, and we alert you to those as well.

Legal lore

Sometimes we pause to explain something: the origin of a word, perhaps, or why a particular piece of legislation was passed. You do not need to know these things to make use of this book, but we hope you find them interesting.

Power points

Sometimes we pause to empower you to do something.

Check out our website

Buying this book gives you the right to use our special readers' website.
www.youneedthisfirst.co.uk

A word of encouragement

In an ideal world, your debtors would cave in and pay up after your first letter. If that happens to you, you are fortunate. It is, however, possible that at some time you will have to sue them. The court stage of debt recovery involves some serious formfilling. *Don't be fazed by the forms.*

Forms were invented to set out at a glance information which might otherwise take a six-page letter, full of irrelevancies, to deliver. The court forms were designed to give the court the information it needs to handle your case, in a format which officials could rapidly and easily understand.

While accuracy is important, formfilling is not an exact science and many people find it hard. Rosy, in particular, complains bitterly that the 'space provided' is always the wrong size for what she wants to say, and that she does not always understand the questions, or finds the instructions ambiguous. She thinks too much, obviously.

Help is at hand for readers like Rosy.

● We explain the claim form, Form N1, in detail. It is vital to get N1 right because it is the form you need to start off a claim for debt in the County Court.

● We provide worked examples of this and the other forms.

- You can print off as many forms as you need from the court service website (www.courtservice.gov.uk). This means you can have as many 'dry runs' as you wish.

- Do not be afraid of telephoning or visiting the court; the officials are used to helping litigants in person – and even lawyers who find forms difficult! – with their paperwork.

- Consider getting your completed paperwork checked by a court official before you file it. It's galling as well as time-wasting to have a good claim returned to you because you've ticked the wrong box or forgotten to sign the form.

- Check out the court service website at www.courtservice.gov.uk which will guide you to the form menu. At the time of writing it is possible to complete most of the forms online, but not to send them electronically.

Clear English or lawspeak?

Wherever possible, we use WYSIWYG words – **w**hat **y**ou **s**ee **i**s **w**hat **y**ou **g**et – in this book; but there are times when we have either to use legal terms or to use ordinary-seeming words in ways which a non-lawyer may find confusing.

Legal documents have traditionally been written in archaic language, because this wording has stood the test of time – often several centuries – and has been hallowed by the courts. What is more, the use of technical language can sometimes enable specialists to express esoteric concepts in a kind of professional shorthand – let's call it lawspeak – which is useful to them but meaningless to others. This idea of a private language is not new, as anyone who has eavesdropped on a group of professionals – plumbers, doctors, accountants, motor mechanics – can tell you; but lawspeak is more arcane than most.

The problem with lawspeak is not so much the Latin and French, however, as its use of English terms which mean different things to lawyers and to non-lawyers – with all the potential for misunderstanding which that entails. Our favourites are *personal service* and *warrant of execution.*

Since April 1999 the courts have made valiant efforts to modernise their language in an effort to become more user-friendly and encourage litigants in person. For example, a plaintiff has become a claimant and a summons has become a claim form. There are still plenty of baffling terms, however, and many court forms, including some of the enforcement ones in this book, are still, at the time of writing, unmodernised. But have no fear! All is made clear in the Buzzwords section below.

Buzzwords

affidavit – a written statement of evidence.

Legal lore

The word *affidavit* comes from Latin *affidare* – to declare (on oath) – and means 'He, she or it has declared'. There. Now you can bore people at parties.

An affidavit has to be signed by the witness and confirmed as true (sworn or affirmed) before a solicitor (who will charge £5) or a court official (who will do it for free). An affidavit is the written equivalent of spoken evidence given in the witness box. Since 26 April 1999 written evidence does not always have to be in affidavit form. We will alert you when you need an affidavit.

attachment of earnings – an order for a *judgment debt* (see below) to be paid by instalments out of the debtor's earnings from employment.

Think of attachment of earnings as private PAYE with you as the taxman.

bailiff – in this context, a court official whose job includes collecting cash, and/or seizing and selling goods, in payment of *judgment debts* (see below).

7

bankruptcy – the situation in which the court declares that a person cannot pay their debts, and the person's affairs are put into the hands of an insolvency practitioner.

After a period of time (usually two years if the debts come to £20,000 or less, three years if it is more than £20,000) the debtor is allowed to keep all new earnings and all new assets. In effect, the debtor's slate is wiped clean, except for assets which the debtor concealed from their creditors and also certain debts (such as maintenance payments) to which bankruptcy does not apply. For a fuller explanation, see page 71.

Additionally, in appropriate cases a debtor can be subject to an incomes payment order – more about this on page 72.

charging order – a court order by which a judgment debt is secured against the debtor's home or other bricks and mortar.

Think of a charging order as a type of mortgage with you in the position of the lender, although you will not get paid by instalments: you have to wait until the property is sold. You can also get a charging order on investment assets such as shares. For a fuller explanation, see page 66.

claimant (formerly *plaintiff*) – in court proceedings, the person doing the suing.

claim form – in court proceedings, an official form setting out what the claimant wants.

conduct money – reasonable travelling expenses to and from court, which the claimant may be asked to pay to a witness or, in certain circumstances, the debtor (for example, to attend an *oral examination* – see below).

The amount of 'reasonable expenses' will equate to the cost of public transport.

counterclaim – in court proceedings, a claim by the defendant against the claimant.

A counterclaim is not the same as a defence, but often operates as if it were.

County Court – the local court for non-criminal claims.

Debt claims under £15,000 must be started in your local County Court (as opposed to the High Court). If the debt claim is £15,000 or more, you can start it in the County Court, or the High Court if you wish (see page 28 below under *Choosing your weapon*).

CVA (company voluntary arrangement) – a private deal for repayment of debts, between a company and its creditors, supervised by an insolvency practitioner.

default judgment – a legal walkover, where the other side either does not reply to a claim or does not defend the whole or part of it.

defendant – in court proceedings, the person being sued.

enforcement – in court proceedings, the legal process by which the claimant enforces payment of a *judgment debt* (see below).

ex parte – a sort of one-sided hearing in the absence of one party; more details on page 69. An ordinary hearing, with both sides present, is *inter partes*. This is a piece of lawspeak which has so far defied modernisation because all lawyers understand what it means and there is really no concise English equivalent.

fast track – in the County Court, the normal track (see *track* below) for claims of more than £5,000 and not exceeding £15,000.

garnishee order – a court order for a debtor's money in a bank or building society account to be paid direct to a claimant to pay a *judgment debt* (see below).

Legal lore

The term *garnishee* comes from the archaic French *garnir*, to warn and has nothing to do with either bouquets garnis or artistically arranged chives on a plate. The garnishee is the holder of the money (referred to below, for simplicity, as 'the bank'), who is 'warned' – ordered by the court, in fact – to hand it over to you instead of to the debtor. You can also get a garnishee order over money that is owed to the debtor by someone else (wonderful in theory, rarely works in practice). For a fuller explanation, see page 62.

High Court – the court (based in London) which may be appropriate for high value and/or complex debt claims. Debt claims under £15,000 cannot be started in the High Court.

instalment order – an order by the court for a debt to be repaid by instalments.

issue – in court proceedings, to put the court's official stamp on your claim form.

IVA (individual voluntary arrangement) – a private deal for the repayment of debts between an individual debtor and their creditors, supervised by an insolvency practitioner. The equivalent for companies is a *CVA* – see above.

judgment – a decision by a court about the merits of a claim. *Note that having a judgment against someone does not guarantee you will get your money.*

judgment debt – a debt for which you have a court judgment in your favour, enabling you, if the money is not immediately forthcoming, to go on to the next stage: enforcement.

letter of claim – a letter to your debtor (see our sample on page 95) warning them of your intention to start legal proceedings if they do not pay up.

—*Always* send a letter of claim before actually suing your debtor. At the time of writing new civil procedure rules are being introduced which will incorporate a 'pre-action protocol' into debt recovery cases. If you do not follow the protocol the judge could penalise you, regardless of whether you won or lost. The main requirement is that you should have made a genuine effort to recover your money before going to court. This means leaping through the various hoops (first reminder, yellow card, etc) and finally the letter of claim. If you do not do so, the court may take the view that your conduct has been unreasonable and reduce or dismiss your claim for costs.

liquidation – similar to bankruptcy, except for companies, not individuals.

The main difference is that the company debtor's slate is wiped clean only if and when it has paid its debts in full (a rare event).

litigant – someone involved in litigation. *A litigant in person* is a litigant who is not represented by a lawyer. And a *litigious* person is someone with a taste for litigation, who sues people at the drop of a hat.

litigation – legal proceedings.

multi-track – in the County Court, the normal track (see *track* below) for claims of £15,000 or more.

nisi (as in *charging order nisi*) – from the Latin word for unless; a sort of provisional court order which, if all goes well, is confirmed (made *absolute*) later.

Official Receiver – the government officer who takes over a bankrupt's financial affairs in the first instance when a bankruptcy order is made. The Official Receiver may subsequently be replaced by a private insolvency practitioner.

oral examination – not a GCSE French test; rather, a question and answer session in court to find out about a debtor's financial situation.

You can't have an oral examination until you have a judgment debt. It doesn't get you the money there and then, but it may give you the information you need to decide what method of *enforcement* (see above) to try.

personal service – the delivery by hand of an important document by leaving it with the recipient (rather than using post, fax, email, etc), because that is what the law requires.

Personal service can be tricky if the debtor is keeping out of the way. To effect personal service you must put the document into the hands of the intended recipient or, if they will not accept it, lay it at their feet. You should also always tell the recipient what the document is, particularly if it is in an envelope. You can always choose to deliver a document by personal service. Although it is sometimes compulsory, personal service is the exception rather than the rule. We will alert you when personal service is required.

petition – in certain proceedings, including bankruptcy, an application to the court.

preferential debts – in the context of bankruptcy/liquidation proceedings, debts which get paid before other unsecured debts.

Example of preferential debts are PAYE, VAT and employees' wages. The fees of the insolvency practitioner looking after a bankrupt's financial affairs are not a debt but a charge on the assets, and are paid before anyone else. For a fuller explanation, see page 29.

Register of County Court Judgments – an official list of judgment debts which were not paid promptly. The list does not include:

● judgment debts which were paid within 28 days of the date of judgment;

● judgment debts which are more than six years old;

● judgment debts where judgment was given in the High Court.

For a fuller explanation, see page 21.

secured creditor – a creditor, for example a mortgage lender, with rights over specific assets of the debtor for the purpose of compelling payment, such rights enabling the creditor to sell the assets if the debtor defaults. See page 29.

service – the legal term for sending or handing over an important document.

small claims track – in the context of debt recovery in the County Court, the track (see *track* below) which deals with debt claims with a financial value not exceeding £5,000.

The procedures on the small claims track are less formal than on the other tracks, so that creditors with small claims can conduct their own cases without legal representation as *litigants in person* (see above).

statutory demand – a formal demand for payment of a debt, as the first stage of bankruptcy or liquidation proceedings.

A statutory demand must be made on the official form and *personal service* (see above) on the debtor, if an individual, is obligatory. For further details, see page 75.

summary judgment – in court proceedings, a quickie judgment, available where the debtor tells the court they will defend, but it is obvious to the court that they have no genuine defence.

track – in the County Court, defended claims are assigned to one of three 'tracks' or sets of procedures, according to value and complexity.

These are the *small claims track* (see above), the *fast track* (see above) and *multi-track* (see above). Small claims track procedures are simpler than the fast track, and so on.

warrant of execution – an authority given by the court for the *bailiffs* (see above) to swing into action.

Frequently asked questions

—**Can I go to court if I can't afford the court fees?**

Yes. You may not have to pay any court fees if you receive:

- income support;
- family tax credit;
- disability working allowance;
- jobseekers' allowance;
- or if paying the court fee would cause you financial hardship.

—**Can it be cost effective to get a debt collection agency or a solicitor to collect my debts for me?**

The answer is a definite maybe.

If you engage a debt collection agency, you will not be able to claim their charges from the debtor unless your contract with the debtor gives you the right to do so. In any case they will usually only threaten and cajole: they are not lawyers and will not normally go to court for you.

If you engage a solicitor to recover a debt of under £5,000, your court claim can include only a modest fixed amount for the solicitor's charges, which are unlikely to cover what you pay out. The small claims track is geared to doing it yourself, but it may still be worth your while to get a professional to do it for you, depending, for example, on how much a professional will charge and the value you put on your own time.

Can I send the boys round?

No. *Harassment of debtors is a criminal offence under the Administration of Justice Act 1970.* Harassment is not limited to violence or the threat of violence, and it can include threats of publicity and demands which by reason of their frequency or aggressive content are designed to alarm or humiliate the debtor. So shopping your debtor to the *News of the World* would probably constitute harassment, and breaking a few windows certainly would.

You can make a personal visit to the debtor, but be polite. There are also special rules for residential landlords, who must not harass their tenants either.

Is non-payment of debts a criminal offence?

No, not usually, and it is a criminal offence to try to extract payment by suggesting that it is.

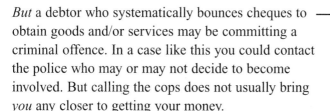

But a debtor who systematically bounces cheques to obtain goods and/or services may be committing a criminal offence. In a case like this you could contact the police who may or may not decide to become involved. But calling the cops does not usually bring *you* any closer to getting your money.

— **Can I take the goods back if they're not paid for?**

Only in exceptional cases, where

- your contract of sale says that the goods belong to you until they are fully paid for, *and*

- the goods remain separate from the debtor's other property and belongings (so you could take back a TV but not a central heating system) *and*

- the debtor gives you permission to take the goods back (you can't force entry onto the debtor's premises), *or* you obtain a court order to do so.

Remember, of course, that if you do take the goods back, they are now second hand and cannot be re-sold as new.

 — **I have repaired the debtor's car. Can I hold onto it until I am paid?**

The good news is yes, you can. And if the debtor still doesn't pay up, you can ultimately get a court order for the bailiffs to sell the car at auction and use the net proceeds towards the debt.

 — The bad news is, it isn't as simple as that. The bailiffs do the selling, not you. That is because you do not own the car, so it is not yours to sell. And of course it may be subject to a finance arrangement, which probably means that, whoever sells the car, the finance house will take its money and leave very little for you.

I am half way through re-roofing a customer's house. The customer won't make interim payments. Can I come off the job until I get some money?

No. Unless your contract gives you a specific right to interim payments, you have to complete the job before you can demand payment.

Do I have to wait before I can sue?

Not always. You have to wait for the period of time which your contract allows for payment (often, for example, 28 days). If your contract entitles you to payment on demand, you can sue immediately you send your invoice

Warning: Be reasonable

See the Power Point on page 12 above. Always observe your pre-action protocol. Even if you win your case, the court may disallow your costs if your conduct has been unreasonable; for example if you have not given the customer written warning (often called a letter of claim – see *Buzzwords* on page 11) of your intention to take them to court.

Do I have to wait before starting bankruptcy proceedings?

No; but the debt must be due and payable immediately. And remember: there is a waiting period built into the procedure – the debtor has 21 days to respond to your statutory demand.

—Can I claim interest on the original debt?

Yes – see under *Interest* on page 39.

 —Can I claim interest on a judgment debt?

Yes, but only if:

● the judgment debt is for not less than £5,000 or

● it is one to which the Late Payment of Commercial Debts (Interest) Act 1998 applies (see page 41 below).

 —Can I claim for my own time/my firm's time in collecting the debt?

No, sorry – not unless your contract with the debtor gives you the right to do so.

 —Can I offer incentives for early payment?

Yes. A small discount, perhaps, or a free tea towel – the choice is yours.

 —I have a judgment debt. Can I pursue more than one method of enforcement at the same time?

The general rule is, yes, but there are exceptions. The main exception is that you cannot, unless the court agrees otherwise, pursue other methods if you already have an attachment of earnings order (see page 57 below).

Remember that *oral examination* (see below) *is not a method of enforcement*, so you can resort to this at any time and it may help you decide how far along the road to pursue your debtor.

Spotting a doubtful customer

You are unlikely to want to supply goods or services, or indeed lend money, to a person who is unwilling or unable to pay you. The best way of avoiding bad debts is to pick your customers with care. If you have serious doubts about a person's willingness or ability to pay, you can check them out.

Much financial information about people is confidential, and is protected by the Data Protection Act 1998. There are, however, sources of information which are publicly accessible.

The Register of County Court Judgments, maintained by Registry Trust Limited of 173/175 Cleveland Street, London W1P 5PE, Tel. 020 7380 0133. For £4.50 a name (make out the cheque to Registry Trust Limited) you can get a printout of any judgments against that name.

But this register does not include High Court ——— judgments (which do not figure on any register), so really big debts can go unrecorded.

The Individual Insolvency Register, which came into operation in March 1999, keeps details of bankruptcy and individual voluntary arrangements (see Buzzwords, page 11). You can apply free of charge:

- *in person* at any official receiver's office (listed in your local telephone directory), where you fill in a form and receive a printout of the information;

- *in writing* to The Insolvency Service, 5th Floor, West Wing, 45-46 Stephenson Street, Birmingham B2 4UP;

- *by telephone* to the Insolvency Service on 020 7637 1110 and they will tell you over the phone whether an *individual* is bankrupt (or is subject to bankruptcy proceedings) or has entered into an IVA.

The Insolvency Service helpline (see above) will also tell you whether a *company* has gone into compulsory liquidation or is subject to liquidation proceedings, or has entered into a company voluntary arrangement (CVA). There is no charge.

The Register of Disqualified Directors, which is held at Companies House – see *Useful Contacts* on page 171 – will tell you free of charge whether someone is on their list of people who are disqualified from acting as company directors.

For more details of all these, see *Useful Contacts* on pages 171–175.

You can also seek information from a licensed credit reference agency, most of which use 'credit scoring systems' and then allocate a pass mark to predict whether or not people are a good credit risk. See the

Yellow Pages for your local agencies, or call Talking Pages on 0800 600 900 for a free nationwide trawl. Using a credit reference agency will of course cost you and may not be totally reliable. In the spirit of research we paid good money for an agency to check out someone who of our certain knowledge had judgments against him, and he came out squeaky clean.

Of course, if you are seriously doubtful about ——— someone's ability to pay, and you don't mind being unpopular, you can ask them to show to your satisfaction where they will get the money – or insist on money up front.

Prevention is better than cure

If you must deal with potentially unreliable customers:

- ask for payment in cleared funds (cash, credit card, electronic transfer, bank draft or building society equivalent) in advance, or on delivery;

- hold onto the goods or the customer's property (for example, the lawnmower which they have handed over to you for repairing) until you are paid;

- ask for, and obtain, security, such as a signed guarantee;

- think carefully about your standard terms and conditions of trade. For example, if you supply goods, do the goods remain yours until they are fully paid for? And if you provide a service, are you entitled to instalments?

Where do I start?

Most debt recovery is a matter of organisation, persistence and good communication. Remember: *Going to court is always a last resort, and involves irrecoverable time and expense.*

Here are the first stages on the road to debt recovery. To make things clearer, we have set this out in the flowchart opposite

Invoice the customer. Make sure the invoice is consistent with your contract, and it is helpful if the invoice re-states the contractual period for payment (such as 28 days) and, if applicable, reminds the customer that you can charge interest. Consider also putting on the invoice a note on what the customer should do if they are unable to pay immediately (such as letting you know at once).

First reminder. We give a sample letter on page 93.

Stiff letter. This is the yellow warning. See our sample letter on page 94.

Ring the debtor. Be polite, be firm and *keep a careful note for your file of what is said and agreed*. You may think you'll remember what was said, but we guarantee

Debt recovery: the early stages

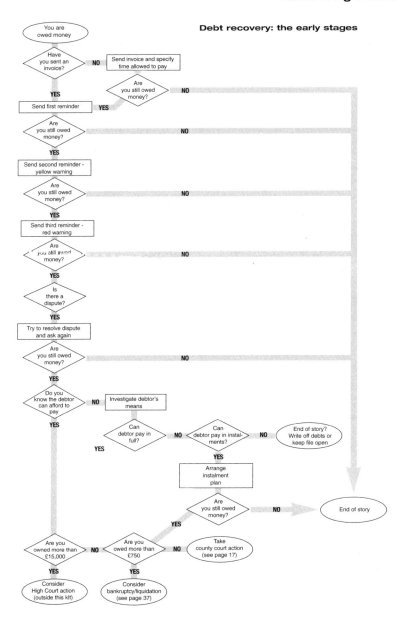

that in a week's time your memory will be as hazy as anyone else's. On-the-spot notes, which professionals call file notes or attendance notes, are an invaluable record and could help you win your case.

Try to find out why you are not being paid and do a deal if you can, for example for payment by instalments (with interest, if chargeable, on the late money). If appropriate, follow up the call with another letter confirming what was said. We give a sample letter on page 96 which sums up the debtor's proposals for payment.

Final warning. The red card! We give a sample letter of claim on page 95.

Ongoing enquiries. From the beginning, try to find out what you can from the debtor about their financial circumstances, such as ownership of property, savings, employment – and of course other debts. Keep good file notes of this information – you may well need them.

Decision time

You have issued your final warning and you still haven't been paid. You need to know why.

Can't pay?

You can't get blood out of a stone. If your debtor is genuinely unable to pay, consider whether any further action would involve throwing good money after bad. But *people's financial circumstances can change*, so:

- keep the file open;
- ask the debtor to provide a statement of means (see our sample on page 100);
- try to persuade the debtor to pay at least nominal instalments;
- review the case periodically in case the debtor comes into money!;
- keep an eye on the time limit for court proceedings. You can't sue on a contract debt more than six years after the date of the contract.

Can pay, won't pay?

There are two possibilities here. We have all met people who are quick to order goods and services but slow to pay for them, and it may be your misfortune to be dealing with one of them.

The second possibility is that the person is withholding payment for a good reason. Do they have a genuine cause for complaint or dispute? If so, you will make the task of collecting the debt a lot easier if you resolve the dispute before you go to court. What's more, it may well be that with the dispute out of the way you will get paid in any case. Consider whether your standard terms and conditions of business should include a complaints procedure (for an example see *The Small Print,* the Simply Legal terms and conditions kit).

Choosing your weapon

If you have security over any of your debtor's assets, now is the time to get your money by realising the security. (You may still need a court order to do this – take legal advice.)

Otherwise, you have two choices:

● court proceedings for recovery of the debt;
● bankruptcy/liquidation proceedings.

Let's consider bankruptcy or liquidation first. Insolvency cramps everyone's style, and members of some professions are actually barred from practising if they are insolvent. The threat of bankruptcy (for an individual) or liquidation (for a company) may therefore concentrate your debtor's mind wonderfully, and you can do the threatening free of charge (see *Sabre Rattling* on page 75), but:

● bankruptcy proceedings are limited to debts of £750 or more, and the same limit (with exceptions) applies to liquidation proceedings;
● bankruptcy/liquidation proceedings are not suitable where the court might find that the debtor has genuine grounds for disputing your claim;

● the threat – particularly the statutory demand (see *Buzzwords* on page 15) – is often more potent than the deed.

This is because taking bankruptcy/liquidation proceedings does not get you to the front of the queue of creditors.

If you have security of some kind, such as bricks and mortar, you may be lucky, because creditors with valid security can realise the secured assets to get their money. All creditors – including secured creditors to the extent that there is a shortfall in their security which they want to make up out of the communal pot – can claim in the bankruptcy/liquidation. But they all have to join the queue.

First in line are the insolvency practitioners, whose fees count as a charge against the bankrupt's assets.

Next come any preferential debts (see *Buzzwords*). They are paid in full before other creditors are even considered.

Then what's left is shared out and all such 'other creditors' are paid proportionately according to the value of their claims. One penny in the pound is not unusual. So, if you bankrupt somebody, you may end up going to a great deal of expense and doing a lot of work for someone else's benefit.

Compared with taking action in the County Court, bankruptcy/liquidation is expensive.

The court fee for a creditor's *bankruptcy* petition is £150. You also have to make an advance payment to the insolvency service of £300, although in theory this may be refundable if the bankrupt's assets allow. For *liquidation* of a limited company, the court fee is £150 and the insolvency service fee is £500.

The other option, County Court action, will be appropriate where:

● The debt is less than £15,000, for which you cannot use the High Court. In practice, a debt claim with a value of less than £50,000 should be started in the County Court, since if it is defended the High Court will transfer it to the County Court anyway.

● The debt is disputed.

● The high costs of bankruptcy/liquidation deter you and/or the debtor's financial situation means you will not get your money by that route. Note also that if the debt is less than £750, the option of bankruptcy/liquidation is in any case not open to you (see above).

● You can see your way clear to *enforcing* your court judgment. There are various means open to you:

- where the debtor is in employment, consider getting an attachment of earnings order;

- where the debtor has valuable belongings, consider calling in the bailiffs;

- where the debtor has savings, consider a garnishee order;

- where the debtor owns their own home or other bricks and mortar, consider a charging order.

We will tell you how to go about all these below: see *Making it stick – enforcement* on page 47.

High Court action (normally outside the scope of this book:) will be appropriate where:

● the debt is of high value (minimum £15,000) and the case is complex;

● you want to use High Court enforcement procedures – see below on judgment debts over £5,000;

One option to bear in mind is to *start* proceedings in the County Court and transfer them to the High Court for enforcement. You must transfer if you want a judgment debt of over £5,000 enforced by seizure and sale of goods. You may also be able to get interest in the High Court where it is not available in the County Court.

In practice, if you as an individual want to use the High Court, you should take legal advice; and companies cannot use the High Court unless they are represented by a solicitor.

See you in the County Court – but which one?

Which court should you use? You can start proceedings in any County Court. You may think that your own local court is the most convenient for you, but it ain't necessarily so.

If the debtor is an individual (that is, not a limited company), it is often more far-sighted to start proceedings in the court *nearest to where the debtor lives* (in other words, the debtor's 'home' court). This is because claims defended by individuals are automatically transferred to the debtor's 'home' court; and oral examinations (see below) and most enforcement procedures have to be carried out there too, however inconvenient this is for you.

If you do not know which is the debtor's 'home' court, your own local County Court can tell you.

You may have to apply to transfer your case to the debtor's 'home' court if:

● the debtor moves house; or

● you want to submit the debtor to an oral examination; or

● you want to enforce your judgment.

You make the application by written request to the court, quoting the case number. There is no special form. Just use our sample letter on page 97.

County court action

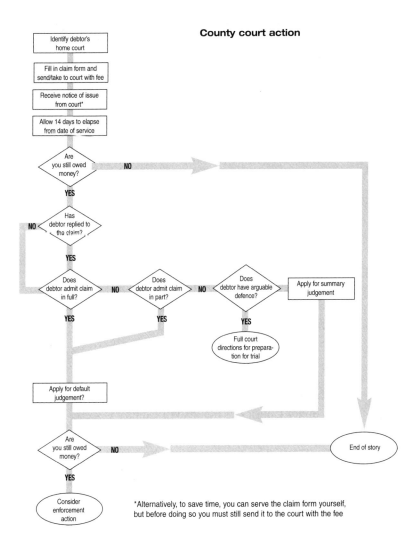

*Alternatively, to save time, you can serve the claim form yourself, but before doing so you must still send it to the court with the fee

If the debtor is a company, the 'home' court is the one nearest the company's principal place of business. Defended claims against companies are not automatically transferred to the company's 'home' court, but for enforcement purposes the 'home' court is often the best place to start proceedings.

The nitty gritty – filling in the claim form

The first thing to do is to fill in a claim form, Form N1. We reproduce a sample form on pages 130–133 and of course you can access it on the website.

The notes on the back of the claim form are clear and helpful, but they cover all types of claims. In our notes below we concentrate on claims for debt.

1. In the...

The name of the court should include the words 'County Court' (eg Eatanswill County Court).

2. Claim no.

Do not fill in the claim number box – the court will allocate a number to your case and fill in this box for you.

3. Claimant

You are the claimant, and this is where you fill in your name and address:

- if you are a sole trader, and use another name for your business, write in your own name, then the words 'trading as', followed by your trade name;

- if you are a firm (two or more people in business together), write in the firm name followed by the words 'a firm';

- if you are a limited company, write the name of the company, including the word 'Limited'.

Insert your business address, and include your postcode, telephone number, fax number and email address if you have one.

If you are under 18, you need an adult, for example a parent, to help you with the claim. The adult is called your litigation friend. After your name, add 'suing by his/her litigation friend' and insert your litigation friend's name. The litigation friend has to fill in another court form (not provided in this book but obtainable from the court), promising to pay any money that the court may order you to pay the debtor in the course of the proceedings (for example, costs).

4. Defendant

On the claim form the debtor is referred to as the defendant. This is where you put the debtor's name and address. Take great care to get their name right:

- if the debtor is an individual, specify Mr/Mrs/Miss/Ms, etc as appropriate, provide first names if you know them, or initials otherwise, and surname;

- if the debtor is a sole trader and uses another name for their business, write in their own name, then the words 'trading as', followed by their trade name;

- if the debtor is a firm (two or more people in business together), write in the firm name followed by the words 'a firm';

- if the debtor is a limited company, give the name of the company and the company registration number. You can get this by doing a free search on the Companies House website (www.companieshouse.gov.uk). While the company number is not obligatory, bear in mind that every company number is unique (like a car registration number or your NI number) and, in a case where several companies had very similar names, quoting the company number could avoid any confusion.

Insert the debtor's address, preferably including the postcode.

- for a private individual, use the debtor's home address;

- for a business debtor, use their principal place of business.

 —If the address is outside England and Wales, take professional advice.

5. Brief details of claim

You can keep this short and simple. Just make it clear that the claim is for payment of money for supply of goods or services.

6. Value

Insert the amount of your claim here, excluding interest and court fees. (The amount you claim in box 8 will include the interest. The court fee goes in at box 9.)

7. Defendant's name and address

There is another box at the bottom of the claim form for the defendant's name and address:

- if you are suing one person only, repeat the name and address of the defendant in this box;

- if you are suing more than one person, you will need a separate form for each defendant. Put in the names of *all* the defendants at the top of each form, and use the box at the bottom of each form to give the name and address of each defendant separately. You will need to repeat all the information about the particulars of the claim on each form.

8. Amount claimed

Insert the value of your claim plus interest at the date of issue of proceedings.

9. Court fee

The court fee is on a sliding scale according to value as follows:

Amount claimed not more than (£)	Fee (£)
200	27
300	38
400	50
500	60
1,000	80
5,000	115
15,000	230
50,000	350
50,000+	500

10. Solicitor's costs

If you are a litigant in person – that is, acting for yourself – you cannot claim solicitor's costs. Put N/A here.

11. Total amount

This is the amount you are claiming, plus the court fee.

12. Issue date

The court will complete the issue date.

13. Particulars of claim

Tell the court how the debt arose. Keep it brief – unless you anticipate the claim will be defended, in which case you need to get your story in first! Give brief details of the contract terms:

● the date of contract;

● the type of contract (whether written or oral);

● the nature of goods or services provided;

● the price;

● other relevant terms – such as time allowed for payment.

You should also provide the invoice number, the date, the invoice amount, the amount of any payments and the balance outstanding.

See our worked example on pages 98–99.

Where the contract is written, you should attach a copy of the contract. In any event, attach a copy of your invoice.

Interest

You won't get interest unless you claim it. You must set out the basis of your claim and your calculation of the amount in the Particulars of Claim. You can get interest

● if your contract with the debtor gives you the right to this;

● if you have a statutory right under the Late Payment of Commercial Debts (Interest) Act 1998. Until November 2000 this Act applied only if the creditor was a small business which supplied goods and services to a large business or public authority – David claiming from Goliath. Now however, the Act is available against small business debtors too. By November 2002 the Act is expected to apply to small and large businesses and the public sector who are claiming from small and large businesses and the public sector.

● at the discretion of the court, under the County Courts Act 1984.

Contractual claim

If you are claiming interest under your contract with the debtor, use the following wording:

'The claimant has a contractual right to interest.

Interest is claimed from: *[insert date, eg 28 days from date of invoice, if that is what your contract specifies]*

Interest is claimed to: *[insert date – which must not be after date of issue of the claim form]*

Interest is claimed on: *[insert amount of debt, before interest]*

Total interest to the date of calculation is: *[insert amount]*

The daily rate of interest after the date of calculation is: *[insert daily rate].*'

Statutory claim – Late Payment of Commercial Debts (Interest) Act 1998

If you are claiming interest under the 1998 Act, the wording to use is:

'The claimant has a right to interest under the Late Payment of Commercial Debts (Interest) Act 1998.'

Then complete as before using an interest rate of 8 per cent (simple) per annum.

Statutory claim – County Courts Act 1984

Insert the following:

'The claimant asks for interest under section 69 of the County Courts Act 1984.'

Then complete as before, again using an interest rate of 8 per cent (simple) per annum.

You will not be awarded two lots of interest on the same amount. Where your claim is for statutory interest, ie under the 1998 or 1984 Acts, you will not be awarded compound interest.

Calculating the daily rate of interest

Using your calculator:

- enter the amount of the debt;
- multiply by the interest rate;
- press the % button;
- divide by 365.

This gives you the daily rate.

For the interest you are owed to date, multiply the daily rate by the number of days the debt has remained unpaid.

14. Statement of Truth

This allows the facts set out in the Particulars of Claim to be treated as evidence. The person signing the statement should write in their name clearly and sign. If you are a limited company, the Statement of Truth should be signed by a director, company secretary or manager, and the signatory's position in the company should be stated.

15. Claimant's or claimant's solicitor's address

This address box is meant for the claimant's solicitor. You do not need to use this box as long as your address on the front of the form is the one you want the court to use.

Now what?

Take or post to the court:

● one copy for the court plus one copy for each defendant; and

● the court fee.

You can pay in cash (in which case use recorded

delivery or deliver personally), or by cheque made out to HMPG (Her Majesty's Paymaster General).

Keep a copy of the claim form(s) for your file.

The court will now – provided you got your formfilling right – issue your claim form (put an official stamp on it) and serve it (see *Buzzwords*) on the debtor.

Service

The court normally posts the issued claim form to the defendant. At the same time, the court sends you a form called *Notice of Issue (Specified Amount) and Request for Judgment* (see *Getting a Default Judgment* on page 46). The form tells you the date of service, ie the date on which, according to the court rules, the debtor is deemed to have received the claim form. According to the court, first class post takes two days. So, if the court posts the claim form, the date of service is two days after posting.

You may be able to speed up the procedure if you are prepared to serve the issued claim form yourself, but:

● a tricky defendant may deny ever receiving the claim form; and

● within seven days after the date of service you *must* notify the court of the date and method of service, using Form N215 (included in this book on pages 134–135). *If you do not send Form N215 to the court you cannot get judgment.*

If you want to serve the claim form yourself, collect the defendant's copy of the issued claim form from the court, or ask them to send it back to you.

You can serve it by:

- delivery to the defendant's address. Personal service (see *Buzzwords*) is not necessary; it is sufficient to put the claim form through the debtor's letterbox. Make a note of the day you delivered the claim form. The date of service, according to court rules, will be the day *after* you delivered the claim form;

- fax – in which case keep your transmission sheet;

- email.

Response time

The debtor must respond within the time limit which the claim form specifies, which – as long as you have filled in the Particulars of Claim on the claim form – is 14 days after the date of service (see above).

The significance of the response time is that if the debtor fails to respond by the deadline, you can get a walkover (see *Getting a Default Judgment* on page 46). So mark the deadline in your diary – and get in quick if the opportunity arises.

What can the debtor do?

The debtor communicates with the court (not with you), although any payments they make will come direct to you.

The debtor can:

- Pay you in full. End of story.

- Admit the full amount of your claim, and offer to pay. You can now apply for a default judgment (see *Buzzwords*) and this may be an attractive option if you find the debtor's payment proposals unacceptable.

- Lie low and say nothing. If the debtor does not respond to the claim form before the deadline, you can apply for a default judgment for the whole amount.

- Admit part of the claim, disputing the balance. You can now apply for a default judgment for the admitted amount only.

- Dispute the whole of the claim. You cannot now apply for a default judgment, but if the debtor's grounds for dispute have, as the court rules put it, 'no real prospect of success', you may still be able to get a summary judgment (see *Buzzwords*).

- Make a claim against you. If so, you may still be able to get a default judgment if the debtor's claim is not a defence to the debt. You will, however, still have to defend the debtor's claim against you (outside the scope of this book; seek professional advice).

- Plus – A slippery debtor can file an acknowledgement of service saying they intend to dispute all or part of the claim. This buys them a breathing space, because they now have 28 days instead of 14 days from the date of service in which to file any defence.

Getting a default judgment

If you are entitled to a default judgment (see above, also *Buzzwords*, page 9), the day after the deadline, complete the Request for Judgment part of the Notice of Issue which the court has sent you.

Think carefully about how you want to be paid. Of course you want the money immediately, but it may be more realistic to accept an offer of instalments. Sign and date the form and return it to the court. There is no fee and you do not have to attend court.

The court will now send you your judgment, and also send copies to the defendant and the Register of County Court Judgments. Well done!

 —Be organised!

- Always quote the case number on all your correspondence with the court.

- Always keep copies of all written communications, both with the debtor and with the court.

- Always keep file notes, with dates, of all meetings and telephone conversations.

Making it stick
– enforcement

The *good* news is that you now have your judgment.
The court has agreed that the debtor owes you the
money, and ordered the debtor to pay you.

The *bad* news is that having a judgment does not
guarantee that you will actually get any money.

If, after you have obtained judgment, you are not paid
promptly, various enforcement procedures are open to
you. Before you take such a step, however, do some
serious thinking. Bear in mind that:

- enforcement will take time and effort on your part;
- there will be further court fees to pay (which get
  added on to the judgment debt, but may of course
  never be recovered).

Is it worth it?

As we have said before, you cannot get blood out of a
stone. A useful first step, therefore, is to find out
whether the debtor has the means to pay. The debtor
may already have provided information about their
means if they have admitted your claim (there is space
for this on the admission form which is provided by the
court).

You can in theory obtain more information informally by writing direct to the debtor, but there is no guarantee that they will reply truthfully or at all. Otherwise, consider an oral examination.

Oral examination

This is a question and answer session before an officer of the court to find out about a debtor's financial situation. First, bear in mind:

- oral examination is not in itself a method of enforcement;

- oral examination is not compulsory before enforcement action;

- oral examination does not get you any money there and then.

But oral examination may give you the information you need to decide which method of enforcement to try. For example, you should be able to find out:

- whether the debtor is in employment and what their earnings are – in which case an attachment of earnings order is an option;

- whether the debtor has any valuable assets, in which case you might consider a warrant of execution;

- whether the debtor owns any bricks and mortar, in which case a charging order is a possibility;

- whether the debtor has savings, in which case you could opt for a garnishee order.

*Since the debtor must verify to the court that the
information that they give in an oral examination is
true, it is more likely to be reliable than would
otherwise be the case.*

Additionally, some people set great store by their
financial privacy. The threat of having to reveal their
secrets is enough to persuade them to pay up. Your
debtor may be one of these.

Procedure

If applicable, apply to transfer the case to the debtor's
'home' court – see above at page 32.

Complete the court request form (N316 Request for
Oral Examination) which you will find on page 130
and on the website.

Prepare to pay the court fee of £40 using cash, postal
order or a cheque made out to HMPG.

Send or take the form and the fee to the debtor's
'home' court. This is the local County Court for the
area where the debtor lives. If you do not know which
court to use, your own local County Court will tell you.

The examination hearing

The court sets a time and date for the oral examination
and notifies both parties.

The examination will be conducted in private by an officer of the court (not usually a judge). The hearing is likely to be relatively informal. All the same, the debtor is under oath.

The way oral examinations are conducted varies from court to court. Ring the court concerned beforehand and find out how they go about it. You can often agree beforehand with the court official which of you will ask the questions. Some claimants prefer the court officer to do so while they take notes.

Failing any input from you, the court uses a standard list of questions based on the *Statement of Means* on page 100. Study the *Statement of Means* and use it as a basis for your questions. You should normally attend, although many claimants do not. Being there in person will also give you an opportunity:

- to press in with 'supplementaries' like 'If money is so tight, how did you manage to pay for the skiing holiday?';

- to see how the debtor reacts to each question: body language can be very revealing.

If you choose not to attend, you should write to the court in advance explaining that you will not be there. You can still send the court specific questions which you want answered in your absence.

What happens if the debtor does not show?

This is a common occurrence and the court gives the debtor the benefit of the doubt first time around. The court sets another time and date for the examination, but this time the debtor's failure to attend without good excuse may amount to contempt of court, for which the sentence could be a short spell in prison.

You do not have to pay another examination fee, but you may, if asked by the debtor, have to give them conduct money (see *Buzzwords*) to travel to court. Pay this money promptly direct to the debtor on request. You can pay what you want, but if you have paid too little and the debtor does not turn up, you may have given the debtor the excuse they need, and the judge may not be able to send them to prison for failing to show up.

No earlier than four days before the new examination date, let the court know in writing, as applicable:

● that the debtor has not asked you for conduct money; or

● that you have paid conduct money – stating the amount and how this was calculated.

What happens if the debtor still does not show?

The court tries again, and this time the court bailiff effects personal service (see *Buzzwords*) of the notice of hearing on the debtor. Failure to attend may now cause the judge to issue a warrant for the debtor's arrest.

Oral examination of a limited company or firm

You can find out about a limited company's financial situation by asking for oral examination of one of its directors. This may require a little gentle sleuthing.

The company's writing paper will often give the names of the directors, but not their addresses. Have no fear! You can find out directors' names and addresses – as well as their occupations, date of appointment and dates of birth – from Companies House. Their general enquiry number from April 2001 is 0870 3333636 There is a fee of £4 – per company, not per director – and they then post or fax the details back to you. They will post you the details for £4, or fax them for £5 (payable over the phone by credit card). Unfortunately, some devious and/or secretive companies name other companies as their directors. In this case, all you will get is the name and address of those companies, which won't help much, especially if they registered offshore.

The oral examination procedure is the same as for an individual debtor, but as a first step you may have to transfer the case to the director's 'home' court if this is not the same as for the company's place of business. (See page 97 for the standard letter asking to do this.)

Where your debtor is a firm or partnership, ask for oral examination of one of the partners.

Warrant of execution

This is an authority from the court to allow the bailiffs to enter the debtor's home or business premises and either collect money to pay the judgment debt or take away the debtor's belongings to sell at auction. In *The Mill on the Floss* by George Eliot (1860), several burly bailiffs force their way into the debtor's home and carry off everything of value.

But bailiffs have changed their methods since then. Today's bailiffs are not allowed to break into the debtor's home, although they can force entry into business premises as long as these do not include residential accommodation (so a debtor living over their shop might be safe).

Once inside, the bailiffs cannot take away:

- *basic household and personal belongings* which the debtor and their family need for day-to-day living. (TVs, videos and hi-fis are not yet regarded as necessities and are therefore fair game);

- *belongings which the debtor needs in order to work* – which can include tools, computers and vehicles (but not one used simply to drive to and from work; so the bailiffs might leave a van but take a car);

- *items which do not belong to the debtor*, or of which the debtor is not the sole owner, or which are on lease or HP;

- *items which are not worth the cost of removing and selling.*

A warrant of execution is a waste of time and money if the debtor has no money and no valuable belongings.

Procedure – County Court

The procedure set out below applies to judgment debts of less than £5,000.

 — Above this figure, you usually need the High Court equivalent (outside the scope of this book).

Complete the court request form N323 which you will find on page 137 and on the website. Note there is space on the form for you to give any information you have about the debtor's belongings and their value. The bailiffs are not detectives and can only work from the information you give them. If you want results, do your homework.

Prepare to pay the court fee, using cash, postal order or a cheque made out to HMPG. The fee is currently £25 where you are seeking to recover not more than £125 and £45 for amounts exceeding £125. If the judgment debt is payable by instalments, you can ask the bailiffs to collect *either* the whole amount of the judgment debt *or* the unpaid instalments, and the fee will be in accordance with the amount you ask the bailiffs to collect.

Send or take the form and the fee to the court where you obtained the judgment.

What happens next?

Within ten working days of receiving your form, the court sends an ultimatum to the debtor – pay the full amount to the court in seven days, or else.

The 'or else' is that if the debtor does not pay, the bailiffs will call and try to collect the money. Failing that, they will try to seize goods for sale at auction.

The court should report to you on the outcome, and if you do not hear from them within, say, a month of sending off your form, you should ring and ask for an update.

If the bailiffs are unsuccessful, the court will tell you why. This is usually because the bailiffs cannot find the debtor, or any of the debtor's belongings, or any belongings worth selling.

Can you ask the bailiffs to try again?

Yes. There is a special form, N445, for this on page 138 and on the website. You can use this to update the information you have given the bailiffs, such as any change of the debtor's address or any new information about their belongings which comes to light. You must also pay an extra fee of £20.

Can the debtor grab a breathing space?

Yes. The debtor can apply to the court to suspend the warrant. Typically, they make a last ditch offer to pay, either in full or by instalments. If this happens, the court will let you know. You must then decide whether to:

- agree the suspension and accept the offer;

- agree the suspension and ask for more – in which case the warrant will be suspended and an officer of the court will decide how much the debtor can pay and order accordingly;

- refuse to agree the suspension – in which case you will have to attend a court hearing to explain your reasons.

(The hearing will be in private, before a district judge – call the judge 'Sir' or 'Madam'.)

A note on 'walking possession agreements'

This is an agreement between the debtor and the bailiff, and is another way for the debtor to grab a breathing space. On the bailiff's first visit, the debtor signs a list of possessions which the bailiffs will allow the debtor to keep, as long as the debt is paid within an agreed time. If the debtor fails to pay, the bailiffs can come back – entering by force if necessary – and seize the goods.

A note on disputed ownership

A not infrequent problem with warrants of execution is that disputes arise about who really owns the goods which the bailiffs seize. Sometimes these disputes result in court proceedings – in which case, take professional advice.

The bailiffs are allowed to seize *jointly owned goods*, in which case the proceeds are divided between you and the other owner, typically the debtor's partner.

Attachment of earnings

This is a court order for a judgment debt to be paid by instalments out of the debtor's earnings from employment. 'Earnings' here includes pensions, but not the state old age or disability pensions. Think of attachment of earnings as private PAYE, with you as the taxman. An employer has to dock the debtor's wages at source. So attachment of earnings is not relevant if the debtor is:

- out of work;
- self-employed;
- a firm (sole trader or partnership);
- a limited company.

Furthermore, you cannot get an attachment of earnings order against a debtor who is a merchant seaman or who is in the army, navy or air force. There are special rules for these people and you will need to take legal advice.

Even if the debtor is in employment, you cannot apply for an attachment of earnings order unless:

● you have a judgment debt for at least £50; and

● if the judgment debt is payable immediately, the debtor has failed to pay it; *or*

● if the judgment debt is payable by instalments, the debtor has fallen behind with the payments.

Is it worth your while?

Just as people on the very lowest incomes pay no tax, the court will not make an attachment of earning order against a debtor who cannot afford to pay.

The court will get the debtor to fill in a statement of means similar to the one on page 100 and will allow the debtor to retain enough income to keep themselves and their family. This is called the 'protected earnings rate'. The court will not make an attachment of earnings order if the debtor's income is less than the protected earnings rate.

If the debtor's income is more than the protected earnings rate, the court will make an attachment of earnings order, but the amount of the instalments will depend upon the debtor's ability to pay.

Procedure

If applicable, apply to transfer the case to the debtor's 'home' court – see the standard letter on page 97 and on the website.

Complete the court request form N337 which you will find on page 139 and on the website.

Prepare to pay the court fee of £50 using cash, postal order or a cheque made out to HMPG.

You do not have to pay a fee if someone else already has an attachment of earnings order against the same debtor and you ask for your debt to be collected under the existing order (called *consolidation* – see page 62 below). So do some checking before you part with your £50. Ask the debtor's home court to search their Attachment of Earnings Index to find out if an attachment of earnings order is already in force. There is no fee for this and you can do it over the telephone.

Send or take the form and the fee to the debtor's 'home' court. This is the local County Court for the area where the debtor lives. If you do not know which court to use, your own local County Court will tell you.

What happens next?

The court tells the debtor either to pay up or to fill in a statement of means form (which the court will supply, and which is similar to ours on page 100). If the debtor does not reply, the court can ultimately order the arrest of the debtor and make them fill in the form at the court.

From the information in the statement of means form, the court calculates the protected earnings rate and, if the debtor's earnings exceed this, the amount of the instalments that will be docked from their wages.

Copies of the order are then sent to:

● the debtor's employer, so that they know how much to deduct and when;

● the Centralised Attachment of Earnings Payments System (CAPS), which will collect the payments and pass them on to you;

● the debtor;

● you.

Can the debtor grab a breathing space?

Yes. The debtor can apply to the court to suspend the order. Many debtors will apply to do so if they do not want their employer to find out they are in debt. Typically, the debtor makes a last ditch offer to the court, to pay the debt direct to you, either in full or by instalments. If this happens, the court will decide whether to suspend the order and you will be informed of their decision.

If the attachment of earnings order is suspended, but

the debtor does not keep up the payments, you can ask the court to reinstate the order. You need yet another form for this, N446, which you will find on page 140 and on the website. There is no fee.

Can you have your say?

Yes. If you think any decision by the court is wrong (for example, because of false information from the debtor), you can ask them to reconsider. This might happen if, for example:

● no attachment of earnings order is made;
● the amount of the instalments seems too low; or
● the order is suspended.

For this, you will need yet another form, N244 (available on the court service website), and you *must* get this back to the court with a fee of £50 within 16 days of the date of the relevant order.

Your request may lead to a court hearing (held in private, before a district judge – call the judge 'Sir' or 'Madam').

What happens if the debtor becomes unemployed?

The attachment of earnings order lapses, but it can be reinstated if the debtor gets another job. You need Form N56, which is also available on the court service website. There is no fee.

What happens if the debtor changes jobs?

You have to find out the name and address of the new employer (not always easy, but consider using an oral examination – see page 48). You can then ask the court to notify the new employer. The form for this is N446 (see above). There is no fee.

A note on consolidated orders

This is the one you can get for free if another creditor has been there before you (see page 59 above). A consolidated order can be made where two or more people have applied for attachment of earnings orders against the same debtor. The effect is to simplify the employer's role. Instead of coping with a multiplicity of orders, the employer takes a single amount from the debtor's wages and sends it to CAPS (see above). The court then sends you your share. Note, however, that the *advantage* of a consolidated order is that there is no up front court fee, although the court deducts 10 per cent of all money received from the employer. The *disadvantage* is that you may well receive less money, less often.

Garnishee order

A garnishee order (see *Buzzwords* for the derivation) is a court order for the debtor's money in a bank or building society account to be paid direct to you to pay a judgment debt. You can also get a garnishee order over money that is owed to the debtor.

You cannot apply for a garnishee order unless:

● you have a judgment debt for more than £50; *and*

● if the judgment debt is payable immediately, the debtor has failed to pay it; *or*

● if the judgment debt is payable by instalments, the debtor has fallen behind with the payments.

And:

● your order will be ineffective unless there is actually money in the debtor's bank at the time the bank receives the garnishee order;

● your order will not catch money which comes into the account after the order is made;

● you cannot get a garnishee order over a joint bank account.

There are two significant problems with garnishee orders:

● Finding out in sufficient detail where the debtor keeps their money. You may for example have the debtor's bank details on cheques which you have received from them previously – but if the cheques bounced in the past, is there really any money there now? (Otherwise, try an oral examination – see page 48 above.)

● Getting at the money before the debtor gets wind of your plans and spirits it away.

So, if a garnishee order is going to work, you need reliable intelligence, immaculate timing and the element of surprise. In theory, a garnishee order is supposed to work like the perfect ambush. In practice, it is more like the Keystone Cops – more often than not, the debtor and the money will be one step ahead of you.

Procedure

Complete the court request form N349 which you will find on page 141 and on the website. Note that the form is in fact an affidavit (see *Buzzwords*), so take care that the information you provide is accurate and remember that you must sign it in front of a solicitor or a court official.

Prepare to pay the court fee of £50, using cash, postal order or a cheque made out to HMPG.

Send or take the form and the fee to the court which is dealing with your case.

As timing is crucial, tell the court the date (ideally the day after the debtor's pay day – you see how important good intelligence is!) on which you want them to make the order.

What happens next?

The garnishee procedure is in two stages.

● The court orders the bank to freeze the money in the debtor's account. This is done without the debtor's prior knowledge (obviously!), but the debtor is sent a copy of the order one week after the event. If the district judge has doubts about your application, you *may* be called in to explain yourself to the district judge.

● The court orders the bank to take money from the debtor's account and pay it to you. Before they make the order, however, there *will* be a hearing before the district judge, which you need to attend. Any hearing will be in private, before a district judge – call the judge 'Sir' or 'Madam'.

If there is no money in the account or it is overdrawn, the bank is expected to notify the court. You will then know you are onto a loser. You should withdraw your application before the hearing. Otherwise, you may have to pay the costs of the debtor and/or the bank. Note that in any case the bank can make an administration charge – currently £55 – for dealing with the garnishee order, and this has priority over your judgment debt. This of course reduces by £55 the amount available to you.

Charging order

This is a court order by which a judgment debt is secured against the debtor's home or other bricks and mortar. Think of a charging order as a type of mortgage with you in the position of the lender, although you are not paid by instalments and will have to wait for your money until the property is sold. You can also get a charging order over investment assets such as shares.

 —It may also be possible to get a charging order over the debtor's pension, although this may not be worthwhile unless the debtor is of pensionable age: take professional advice.

By contrast to a garnishee order (where you are shooting at a moving target), a charging order is aimed at assets such as bricks and mortar, which may be harder for the debtor to conceal or dispose of quickly. The exception is, of course, shares, which can be sold instantly.

Do you really want a charging order?

Consider:

● The property may already be heavily mortgaged. An oral examination (see page 48) will tell you more about this.

- The court may not be willing to grant a charging order for a small judgment debt.

- The debtor may not be the sole owner of the property. You can still get a charging order, *but only over the debtor's share of the property.* And it is much more difficult to enforce sale without the co-owner's agreement – take professional advice.

Do you really want to do it yourself?

Consider:

- In practice, the procedures are complicated and it would be a reasonable decision to get a lawyer to act for you. For example, you will usually need details of the property from HM Land Registry and the application is inevitably more complicated where the debtor is a co-owner of the property.

- The charging order is only the first stage – it only prevents the debtor from selling the property; it doesn't pay you off. You still need a separate order for sale (outside the scope of this book) before you get your money.

Procedure

Apply to HM Land Registry for details of the debtor's property. You first need the title number for the property – apply on Land Registry Form 96, obtainable from your local Land Registry (see below).

—Once you have the title number, you can apply for a copy of the register for the property, including the filed plan (ie the Land Registry's official plan of the property). Use Land Registry Form 109 (see below). Copies of the register are known as office copy entries. The Land Registry fees are £4 for each office copy entry and £4 for each copy of the plan. You have to apply to the Land Registry which deals with the property. To find out which branch this is, telephone HM Land Registry on 020 7917 8888 and press 1 for general enquiries. Or go to their website on www.landreg.gov.uk.

—Not all properties are yet registered. If it transpires that the property concerned is unregistered, you will need to have the debtor orally examined to get the information you need. Take professional advice.

Apply for a charging order nisi (see *Buzzwords* on page 8) and provide an affidavit in support, examples of which you will find on page 112 and on the website. Take care that the information you provide is accurate and remember that you must sign it in front of a solicitor (who will charge a small fee) or a court official (who will do it for free).

Prepare to pay the court fee of £50, using cash, postal order or a cheque made out to HMPG.

Send or take the affidavit and the fee to the court which is dealing with your case.

What happens next?

The charging order procedure is in two stages.

Stage 1

The court puts a temporary charge (a 'charging order nisi' – see *Buzzwords*) on the property, which will remain in force until there is a hearing. The charging order nisi is made *ex parte* (see *Buzzwords*) – in the debtor's absence and without notice.

The court sends you copies of the charging order nisi which gives you a date for the hearing, and also copies of your affidavit.

Not less than seven days before the hearing date, you must serve one copy of the order and of your affidavit on the debtor. You must also serve copies on anyone else with a mortgage or charge over the property.

You MUST also serve the papers on any co-owner of 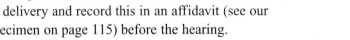 the property (usually a spouse or partner). Personal service is not necessary: first class post is sufficient, but keep a note of the date, time and place of posting or delivery and record this in an affidavit (see our specimen on page 115) before the hearing.

You attend the hearing. This will be in private, before a district judge – call the judge 'Sir' or 'Madam'.

As soon as you have your charging order nisi, it is prudent (though not compulsory) to register it with HM Land Registry. This prevents the debtor from selling the property and pocketing the proceeds, as there could be a longish delay between your charging order nisi and charging order absolute.

Send to the Land Registry which is local to the property

● a copy of the charging order nisi

● a cheque for £40

● a form CT2

Form CT2 is a statutory declaration and needs to be sworn (see *Buzzwords*).This will cost you £5 to swear before a solicitor; this is one document you cannot swear before a court official.

To find out which branch to apply to, telephone HM Land Registry on 020 7917 8888 and press 1 for general enquiries. Or check out www.landreg.gov.uk.

Stage 2

If your application is successful, the court converts the temporary order (nisi) into a permanent charging order, called a charging order absolute. To protect your position prior to sale, you should register the charging order absolute with the Land Registry if you have not already done so (see above).

A final note on enforcement in general

If in the course of any enforcement you receive money direct from the debtor, *always tell the court.*

Bankruptcy

Legal lore

In medieval Italy, a moneylender who could not pay his debts had his bench or counter – his *banco – rupt*ured or broken by his creditors. He was put out of business.

Today, a bankruptcy order is a formal declaration by the court that an individual is insolvent. The effect is that the bankrupt person's financial affairs are put into the hands of an insolvency practitioner, who collects in the bankrupt's assets and shares them out among the creditors.

After a period of time (two years minimum if the total debts come to £15,000 or less, three years if they are £20,000 or more) the debtor is allowed to keep all new earnings and all new assets. In effect, the debtor's slate is wiped clean, except for assets which the debtor concealed from their creditors and also certain debts (such as maintenance payments) to which bankruptcy does not apply.

In the meantime, during the bankruptcy, there are restrictions on the bankrupt's financial activities. But today's bankrupt, unlike the Italian moneylender, can still continue to earn their living (with certain restrictions – a bankrupt cannot be a company director, practise as a GP or a solicitor or be an MP, for example) as long as they use their own name and do not borrow (the official term is 'pledge credit for') more than £250 without telling the lender about their bankruptcy. And today's bankrupt keeps their bench – that is, the tools of their trade – and also basic household and personal belongings which the bankrupt and their family need for day to day living.

Legal lore

What, you may ask, happens if an undischarged bankrupt is earning megabucks? Can they keep it all? Well, the court can, where appropriate, make an *incomes payment order* against a bankrupt whose earnings during the bankruptcy period justify this. A recent case involved a famous sportsman who went spectacularly bankrupt. He generated a lot of media attention and made a lot of money appearing on chat shows and working as a commentator. The court made an incomes payment order against him and the proceeds went to his creditors.

Note that the court will not make an incomes payment order which would reduce the bankrupt's income below what is seen to be the reasonable domestic needs of the bankrupt and their family.

Normally an incomes payment order ceases when the debtor is discharged from their bankruptcy.

Note that you can use bankruptcy procedure in two ways:

- as an alternative to a court claim for debt; or
- as a method of enforcing a judgment debt.

Do you really want to bankrupt your debtor?

'Can pay, won't pay' debtors (see page 27), particularly those in business or a profession, are the likeliest target. Bankruptcy would cramp their style and they would prefer to avoid it. The *threat* of bankruptcy, in the form of a statutory demand (see *Buzzwords* and also page 75 below), involves no court fees and may well make the debtor pay up in order to stay in business.

But this threat doesn't work with everyone. A real no-hoper may welcome bankruptcy. They have been in deep trouble financially for a long time. Now you come along and save them the cost of bankrupting themselves! This is currently a £120 court fee – waived if they are on benefits – plus £250 compulsory Official Receiver's deposit – all payable in cash to the court (well, would you accept a cheque from a potential bankrupt?). In two or at most three years' time they will be discharged, and they will be free to start again with a clean slate.

While the *threat* of bankruptcy may concentrate your debtor's mind wonderfully and get you a quick result, bear in mind:

- bankruptcy proceedings are limited to debts of £750 or more. If you are owed less than £750 you can gang up with other small creditors to get over the £750 hurdle.

- bankruptcy proceedings are not suitable where the debtor has genuine grounds for disputing your claim;

- taking bankruptcy proceedings does not get you to the front of the queue of creditors.

Creditors with valid security (shares, bricks and mortar and so on) are the lucky ones. They can realise the secured assets to get their money. All creditors – including secured creditors to the extent that their security is worth less than the amount they are owed – can claim in the bankruptcy, but their position in the queue is rigidly defined.

After the insolvency practitioner has received his fees and the preferential debts (see *Buzzwords*) have been paid in full, the rag, tag and bobtail are paid proportionately from what's left, according to the value of their claims.

So, if you bankrupt somebody, you may be going to a lot of effort and expense for someone else's benefit (and even – see above – the bankrupt's benefit).

We mentioned expense, above. Compared with suing for debt in the County Court, bankruptcy proceedings are expensive. The court fee for a creditor's (as opposed to a debtor's) bankruptcy application is £150. You also have to make an advance payment to the Insolvency Service of £300, although in theory this may be refundable later if the bankrupt's assets allow. So you will have to pay out £450 with no guarantee of any return on your money.

Additionally, your £300 is refunded if no bankruptcy order is made and the petition is withdrawn. The obvious scenario would be if the debtor paid you in full.

Sabre Rattling – the statutory demand

A statutory demand says 'Pay up – or else!'

It is a formal demand for payment of a debt, as the first stage of bankruptcy proceedings. A statutory demand must be made on the official form; and personal service (see *Buzzwords* again) on the debtor is obligatory.

Personal service doesn't mean serving the document yourself. You can arrange this with a process server (look in the Yellow Pages under Detective Agencies). The court is not involved at this stage.

You do not *need* to serve a statutory demand if you already have a judgment debt (see *Buzzwords*) *and* you have issued a warrant of execution (see *Buzzwords* on page 15) *and* the bailiffs have entered the debtor's premises but come away empty-handed. You can still, however, choose to do so, and as this exception is of limited scope it is in fact sensible always to do so.

Given that the *threat* of bankruptcy is often more effective than the bankruptcy order itself (see above), serving a statutory demand on a debtor is always a useful way to build up the pressure. Unless you pay a process server to do it for you, serving a statutory demand costs you nothing – there is no court fee at this stage. Some creditors might use the time and place of service to embarrass the debtor. You can probably think of several times and places which would have the desired effect.

— Beware! Before you serve a statutory demand, be sure that the debtor cannot challenge the validity or amount of the debt. If the debtor makes a successful court application to set aside (ie cancel) your demand, you will usually end up paying the debtor's legal costs in the case as well as your own. These may be substantial if there is a lengthy court hearing. If the debtor makes an application to set aside your demand, take legal advice immediately.

Procedure – the statutory demand stage

Fill in the official form (Form 6.1; 6.2 if you already have a judgment against the debtor). You will find both forms in this book on pages 142 and 146 and on the website, together with a worked example. *You must use* *the correct form – nothing else has the legal clout you need.* Fill the form in carefully, and bear in mind:

1. You cannot claim for any debt to the extent that it is secured (eg if you have the benefit of a mortgage over the debtor's property).

2. The Particulars of Debt must state

● when the debt was incurred;

● how it arose; and

● the exact amount due at the date of demand;

● it is sensible to include a calculation, and to attach copies of relevant contracts or invoices.

3. You have to include the name and address of the court which will deal with the case. This is usually the debtor's local County Court, but check with the court whether they deal with bankruptcies – not all County Courts do. If they do not, they will tell you where to go. County Courts are listed in the telephone directory under Courts.

A note on London: If, for the greater part of the previous six months, the debtor has lived or carried on business in the 'London Insolvency District', you must start proceedings in the High Court. The London Insolvency District, broadly speaking, comprises the City of London, the City of Westminster and the London boroughs.

If you think this may apply to your debtor, you can check whether you should be using the High Court by telephoning the Bankruptcy Section on 0207 936 6448. And, if the High Court does have jurisdiction, the address to put on your statutory demand is: The Bankruptcy Court, Royal Courts of Justice, Thomas More Building, The Strand, London WC2A 2LL.

Although High Court proceedings are generally outside the scope of this book, have no fear! For straightforward bankruptcy matters the procedures and fees are the same as for County Courts, and you can use the forms provided with this book and on the website. The main difference is that bankruptcy petitions in the High Court have to be filed *in person*, not posted. See *High Court Procedure* below.)

4. You have to sign the form – and the signature must be that of an individual (not a trade name, etc).

5. You have to date the form – in practice, put this in shortly before service.

Now effect personal service (see *Buzzwords*). To do this, you (or your process server – see below) must leave the statutory demand with the debtor. In practice this means handing it to the debtor or, if they will not accept it, laying it at their feet. You should tell the debtor what the document is, particularly if it is in an envelope. If you do not want to effect personal service yourself, arrange for a competent process server with professional indemnity insurance (look in the Yellow Pages under Detective Agencies) to do it for you.

If your debtor is keeping out of the way and you cannot find them, there are alternative procedures for service which are outside the scope of this book. Take professional advice.

Take a note of the precise date, time and venue of service, and incorporate these details into an affidavit of service (Form 6.11 on page 150 of this book and on the website). If you instruct a process server, make sure they provide a completed affidavit of service for you. The affidavit must be signed in front of a solicitor or court official.

What happens next?

The debtor has 21 days from the date of personal service to respond to your statutory demand. The debtor has four options:

● Pay up in full. End of story.

● Apply to the court within 18 days for the statutory demand to be set aside – the obvious response if the debt is disputed. This will lead to a court hearing. Take professional advice.

● Apply for an individual voluntary arrangement – often abbreviated to IVA (see *Buzzwords*) – a private deal for the repayment of debts between an individual debtor and their creditors, supervised by an insolvency practitioner. People with IVAs are allowed to carry on trading. An IVA application has the effect of putting bankruptcy proceedings on hold.

Further details are outside the scope of this book.

● Lie low and say nothing – in which case you need to consider whether you want to go on to bankruptcy proceedings.

Procedure – the bankruptcy stage

Check with your nearest County Court whether they deal with bankruptcies (not all do). If they do not deal with bankruptcies, they will tell you where to go.

Check that your debtor is not already bankrupt or about to become bankrupt. You can do this by telephoning the Individual Insolvency Register (see *Useful Contacts* on page 173).

Allow 21 days to pass, then check with the court whether the debtor has applied either to set aside your demand or to obtain an IVA.

At the same time, check with the court whether there is already a bankruptcy petition in existence – and if there is, do not continue with your own petition. Instead, contact the existing petitioner.

Fill in the bankruptcy petition (Form 6.7) which you will find on page 151 and on our website. Use the worked example on page 117 as a guide. Fill it in carefully.

Fill in the affidavit of truth of statements in bankruptcy petition (Form 6.13 on page 153 and on our website),

which provides the evidence to back up your petition.
Use our worked example as a guide. If more than four
months have passed since you served your statutory
demand, you must explain the reason for the delay. As
the form is an affidavit, remember that you must sign it
in front of a solicitor (who will charge a small fee) or a
court official (who will do it for free). If you have not
already done so, you must do the same with your
affidavit of service of the statutory demand.

Prepare to pay the court fee of £150 and the Official
Receiver's fee of £300. You make one payment of £450,
using cash, postal order or a cheque made out to
HMPG.

Send or take (note that the High Court *insists* on the
latter) the following documents to the court which is
dealing with the case:

- bankruptcy petition (Form 6.7) plus two copies;
- affidavit of service of statutory demand (Form 6.11)
  plus one copy;
- affidavit in support of the bankruptcy petition (Form
  6.13) plus one copy;
- the fee.

Make sure you keep a copy of everything for your own
file.

If your paperwork is in order, the court will issue your
petition, that is, put an official stamp on it, and give it

back to you for personal service on the debtor.

Effect personal service of the petition on the debtor (see above), and at the same time give the debtor a copy of the affidavit in support of the petition (Form 6.13).

Fill in your affidavit of service of the bankruptcy petition (Form 6.17). As before, this must be signed in front of a solicitor or a court official.

High Court procedure

There are two points to note if you are taking bankruptcy proceedings in the High Court (see *A note on London* on page 77).

The High Court still expects you to file your petition and accompanying documents in person, and not to post them (although this no longer appears to be an express requirement of the rules).

The High Court requires you to check there have been no bankruptcy petitions against the debtor within the previous three years and, if there have, that any such petitions have been dismissed. (The Insolvency Service can tell you only about actual bankruptcies, not near misses.) You need to obtain this information from the High Court's own database, for which you will be charged £5. Here's how:

- Go to the information desk, collect a free map and ask for the Fees Room. There you pay £5 and receive a search ticket.

- Take your ticket to the Thomas More Building, second floor, Room 211. You will be allotted 15 minutes at a computer terminal.

- Armed with your search result, you can then file your petition in the same room. Ask the staff to check your paperwork for you.

Some County Courts may also require this information – practice varies from court to court. Most will do a free search for you either over the telephone or by post. Ask!

What happens next?

The court sets a hearing date for the petition. You must attend – take copies of all the paperwork with you.

Additionally, the court will want to know whether the debt is 'still due and owing'. You can reassure them by bringing with you a Certificate that Debt is Still Due and Owing, which we reproduce below.

CERTIFICATE that debt still due and owing
For petition hearings only

NAME OF DEBTOR:
PETITIONING CREDITOR:

I certify that . . . . to the best of my knowledge and belief the debt on which the petition is founded is still due and owing and has not been paid or secured or compounded for . . . .

Dated   *(Signature)*
                                                         Petitioning Creditor

You should also take with you to the hearing a list of creditors, which we reproduce below. Obviously, if you are the only creditor intending to appear, you will say so on the form.

LIST OF CREDITORS intending to appear on the hearing of the bankruptcy petition

IN THE [HIGH COURT OF JUSTICE
of . . . . . . COUNTY COURT]
No. . . . . . of 20 . .

In Bankruptcy
Re A. B. (name of debtor as in title of petition)
In the matter of a bankruptcy petition file on . . . . 20....
The following Creditors have given notice that they intend to appear on the hearing of the above-mentioned petition on . . . . . . 20 . .

Name of creditor	Address of creditor	Amount owed to creditor	Creditor's Solicitors	Whether intending to support or oppose the petition

[Solicitors for the] Petitioning Creditor (*insert name and address*).

The hearing will be in private, before a district judge – call the judge 'Sir' or 'Madam'. The court will inform you beforehand if the debtor decides to defend the petition, in which case you should take professional advice.

— Note that if your petition is unsuccessful and the court does not make a bankruptcy order, you may be liable to pay the debtor's legal costs.

If you are successful, however, and a bankruptcy order is made, you cannot ask the bankrupt to pay you direct. You have to apply to the Official Receiver, or whoever else is appointed to manage the bankrupt's financial affairs.

Liquidation

Liquidation is to companies what bankruptcy is to individuals. The essential considerations are the same. In particular:

- the threat of liquidation, in the form of a statutory demand, is usually more effective than the proceedings themselves, and much cheaper;

- liquidation proceedings are not suitable where the debtor has genuine grounds for disputing your claim;

- liquidation does not get you to the front of the queue of creditors.

Liquidation is different from bankruptcy in the following respects:

- The £750 minimum level of debt does not apply if you already have a judgment debt against the company debtor; and you have failed to get satisfaction through enforcement procedures (but ask yourself if it would ever be cost effective taking liquidation proceedings for a debt of less than £750).

Do not, however, seek to liquidate a company owing you less than £750 without taking legal advice: the applicable law is even more arcane than usual.

- There is no facility for the company debtor to apply to the court to set aside any statutory demand. Instead, the company can apply to the court to restrain presentation of the petition.

- You do not need to serve a statutory demand, and you may choose not to do so if time is of the essence (the company debtor has 21 days to pay after the demand is served).

- If you do choose to serve a statutory demand it must be left at the company's registered office (see below). Personal service on a director or other senior officer of the company is incorrect.

- County Courts have jurisdiction only where the company debtor's paid up share capital does not exceed £120,000.

- The County Courts in the London Insolvency District (see page 77) do not have jurisdiction to hear company liquidations, and the application has to be started in the High Court. Although High Court proceedings are generally outside the scope of this book, have no fear! For straightforward matters the procedures and fees are the same as for County Courts, and you can use the forms provided with this book and on our website. The address is in Useful Contacts on page 174 under Insolvency in London.

The statutory demand stage

Fill in the official form (Form 4.1) which you will find on page 155 and on our website. Follow the guidelines for 'the statutory demand stage' on page 76 above. Also, make sure you get the name of the company exactly right – which must be the same as the name registered at Companies House – see *Useful Contacts* on page 171.

Effect service of the demand by leaving it at the company debtor's registered office. You may later have to prove this was done, so do not send by post. To be safe, take the demand round personally and put it through the letterbox, keeping a note of the time and date you do so. Otherwise pay a process server to do it for you and make sure they give you an affidavit of service.

The registered office is often different from the company's trading address, but it has to be in England or Wales. To find out a company's registered office address, call Companies House – see *Useful Contacts* on page 171.

Belt and braces – If the registered office address is obviously not a trading address for the company, deliver or post a copy of the demand to their trading address as well.

The liquidation stage

Allow 21 days to pass.

Check to see if someone else has already filed a petition. You do this by searching the Central Index (details in *Useful Contacts* on page 171). If the answer is yes, contact the petitioner.

If there is no prior petition, fill in your petition, using Form 4.2 which you will find in this book and on the website. The information about the company required under headings 1 to 4 inclusive is all available from Companies House.

Fill in the affidavit verifying winding-up petition (Form 4.3, see page 164 and our website), which provides the evidence to back up your petition.

For liquidation of a limited company, the court fee is £150 and the Insolvency Service fee is £500. You make one payment of £650, using cash, postal order or a cheque made out to HMPG.

Send or take the following documents to the court which is dealing with the case:

- statutory demand (Form 4.1) plus one copy;
- winding-up petition (Form 4.2) plus three copies (one for the company, one for the court and two for you);

- affidavit verifying winding-up petition (Form 4.3) plus one copy;

- the fee.

If your paperwork is in order, the court will issue your petition, that is, put an official stamp on it, and give you back three copies (one for you to keep, one for you to serve, and one for you to enclose with your affidavit of service – see below).

Effect personal service (see *Buzzwords*) of the petition on the company debtor. In the case of a company, personal service means leaving the petition with a director or other officer or employee of the company. You should do this at the company's registered office, but if that is not practicable (for example because the company does not carry on business from the registered office) you should effect personal service at the company's principal place of business. At the same time give them a copy of your affidavit in support.

Immediately after serving the petition, you must send the court an affidavit of service. There are two forms:

- use Form 4.4 if you served at the company's registered office;

- use Form 4.5 if you served at the company's principal place of business.

We provide both in this book (see pages 166–167) and on the website – make sure you use the correct one. A sealed copy of the petition must be included as an exhibit with your affidavit.

You must also advertise the petition in the *London Gazette* – on one occasion only. The advertisement must appear not less than seven 'business days' after the petition has been served on the company, and not less than seven 'business days' before the hearing date. A 'business day' is any Monday to Friday, excluding Christmas Day, Good Friday and Bank Holidays – for practical purposes, any day on which the County Court office is open. The *London Gazette* comes out every weekday.

Send the advertisement (see our sample on page 120), together with your cheque for £26.81 inclusive of VAT (details in *Useful Contacts* on page 168). Tell them the date you wish the advertisement to appear and remember to give them at least two days' notice.

Finally, you need to file a certificate of compliance (see our sample on page 127) with the court at least five days before the hearing date, together with a cutting from the *London Gazette* showing your advertisement. This shows the court that you have jumped through the appropriate hoops.

What happens next?

The procedures and outcomes are essentially the same as for bankruptcy – see 'What happens next?' on page 79 above, except that no Certificate of Continuing Debt is required, although you will still need to file a list of creditors.

Sample letters and forms

The documents which follow are examples only, and they appear on the website associated with this book. Any fictitious details are highlighted for you to change according to your needs.

Contents List

Page 93   First reminder
Page 94   Yellow warning
Page 95   Red warning – Letter of Claim
Page 96   Summing up debtor's proposals for payment
Page 97   Asking the court to transfer the case to the
          debtor's home court
Page 98   Sample Particulars of Claim
Page 100 Statement of Means
Page 110 Application for charging order nisi
Page 112 Affidavit in support of application for
          charging order nisi
Page 115 Affidavit of service
Page 125 Advertisement of winding-up petition
Page 127 Certificate of compliance (liquidation)

First reminder

From Pickwick Papers Limited
to Mr R Nupkins
[date]

Dear Mr Nupkins

Stationery Supplies

I refer to my company's invoice of [date] for £____
in respect of stationery supplied to your firm. Under
our standard terms of business, payment should have
been made within 28 days of the date of invoice. We
are entitled to interest for late payment.

Would you please settle this bill within the next seven
days. You should of course ignore this letter if you have
paid us before it reaches you.

Yours sincerely

Samuel Pickwick
Director
Pickwick Papers Limited

Yellow warning

From Pickwick Papers Limited
to Mr R Nupkins
[date]

Dear Mr Nupkins

Stationery Supplies

I refer to my company's unpaid invoice of [date] for
£____ in respect of stationery supplied to your firm.
I am concerned that you have not responded to my
reminder of [date].

Could you please settle this bill within seven days. If
you have difficulty in paying, please contact me
immediately.

Yours sincerely

Samuel Pickwick
Director
Pickwick Papers Limited

Red warning – Letter of Claim

From Pickwick Papers Limited
to Mr R Nupkins
[date]

Dear Mr Nupkins

Stationery Supplies – Unpaid Bill

I refer to my company's invoice of [date] for £____
in respect of stationery supplied to your firm; and to
my reminders of [date] and [date], to which you have
not replied.

I must ask you to settle this bill within the next seven
days. If you fail to do so, I shall take legal action
against you without further warning to recover the debt
together with interest and costs. You should note that
County Court judgments are registered and may make
it difficult for you to obtain credit in the future.

If you have difficulty in paying, please contact me
immediately.

Yours sincerely

Samuel Pickwick
Director
Pickwick Papers Limited

Summing up debtor's proposals for payment

From Pickwick Papers Limited
to Mr R Nupkins
[date]

Dear Mr Nupkins

Stationery Supplies – Unpaid Bill

I refer to our telephone conversation of [date]. You told me that you had been off work with an injured hand (unfortunately, the one you sign cheques with; and your firm has no other authorised signatory). I am glad that you are now recovered and back at your desk.

You offered to pay the debt by instalments of £____ per month starting on [date] and to provide post-dated cheques for the purpose. I am agreeable to this arrangement, provided you keep up the payments. If you fail to do so, the whole amount owed will immediately become due and payable. The unpaid balance will bear interest at a rate of ____% per annum.

I look forward to receiving the first payment and the post-dated cheques.

Yours sincerely

Samuel Pickwick
Director
Pickwick Papers Limited

Asking the court to transfer the case to the debtor's home court

Sadly, Mr Nupkins failed to keep his promises and Mr Pickwick had to sue him in the County Court. He started the case off in his home court but later needed to transfer the case to Mr Nupkins's home court.

From Pickwick Papers Limited

To the Court Manager, Eatanswill County Court
[address]
Claim No.
[date]

Dear Sir
Pickwick v Nupkins, Claim No.

I should be grateful if you would kindly transfer this claim to the Scoffantipple County Court, which is Mr Nupkins's local County Court. Thank you for your assistance in this matter.

Yours faithfully

Samuel Pickwick
Director
Pickwick Papers Limited

Sample Particulars of Claim (page 2 of Form NI)

These particulars of claim assume that the debt is contractual. You should give brief details of the contract terms:

- the date of contract;
- the type of contract (whether written or oral);
- the nature of goods or services provided;
- the price;
- other relevant terms, such as time allowed for payment.

You should also provide the date of invoice, the amount of any payments made and the balance outstanding. If you are claiming interest, you must say so.

Where the contract is written, you should attach a copy of the contract. In any event, attach a copy of your invoice.

In the example below, Pickwick Papers Limited is claiming from Mr Nupkins the sum of £500 representing the amount he owes for stationery which Pickwick Papers Limited have supplied to him.

Claim No. [court to insert]

Particulars of Claim

The claimant is a stationery retailer. By a written agreement dated 1 June [insert year] (copy attached) the claimant agreed to supply the defendant with 30 reams of perfumed paper for £600 inclusive of VAT. The claimant duly supplied the paper and invoivced the defendant on 1 July [insert year] under invoice no. PP2000 (copy attached).

On August [insert year] the defendant paid £100, but despite repeated request for payment, the defendant has not paid the balance of the invoice.

The claimant has a contractual right to interest under clause [ ] of the agreement at a rate of 12%. Interest is claimed from: 29 July [insert year] to today, 28 December [insert year] being 153 days. Total interest to today is: £25.15. The continuing daily rate of interest from today is 16p.

The claimant asked for:

1.   The sum of £500.00.

2.   Interest of £25.15.

3.   Continuing interest at a daily rate of 16p until judgment or earlier payment.

Statement of means

You can ask the debtor to complete this form voluntarily at any stage, or you can use the form as the basis of questions in an oral examination.

The law on data protection restricts the use that can be made of information of the kind you are seeking here. In particular, data must be adequate, relevant and not excessive to the purpose for which it is obtained. We have worded the note at the top of the form on the basis that you will use the information solely in connection with the recovery of money owed to you. If this is not the case, you ought to contact the Data Protection Registrar (details in *Useful Contacts*).

Statement of means

We will use any information you supply to us on this form exclusively in connection with the recovery of money which you owe us, and will otherwise treat it as confidential.

1. Personal details

Debtor's name

Address

Telephone (day)   (evening)

Age

Status: married/cohabiting/single/other (please specify)

Number of children ____Ages of children____

Other dependants____

2. Employment status

2.1 Employed

Employer's name

Employer's address

Job title

Annual wage or salary

2.2 Self-employed

Name of business

Business address

Nature of business

Annual earnings

2.3 Unemployed

Nature of last job

Length of time out of work

2.4 Pensioner

Name of pension provider(s) Yes/No

Annual amount of pension(s)

2.5 Other

3. **Assets**

   3.1 Home

   Do you own your own home? Yes/No

   If yes:

   Are you the sole owner? or co-owner?

   Value of home

   Amount of mortgage

   Name of mortgage lender

   3.2 Vehicles

   Do you own a car or other motor vehicles?

Yes/No

   If yes, please complete the following details for each vehicle you own:

Make

Registration no.

Is vehicle on finance? Yes/No

If yes, please give details in section 4, below.

3.3 Bank details

Do you have a bank account? Yes/No

If yes, please complete the following details for each account:

	1	2	3
Bank name			
Bank address			
Account name			
Account number			
Balance			

3.4 Savings and investments

Do you have any savings or investments?

Yes/No

If yes, please provide details including value

3.5 Property

Do you own property other than your home?

Yes/No

If yes, please provide the following details for each property:

	1	2

Are you the sole owner?

or co-owner?

Value of home

Amount of mortgage

(if any)

Name of mortgage lender

3.6 Pensions

Do you or your employer pay into a pension

scheme? Yes/No   If yes, please give details

Do you receive income from a pension which you
have not declared at 2.4? If so, please give details
here.

3.7 Other assets

Please provide details of any other assets you own, e.g.
boats, jewellery, works of art etc.

3.8 Money owed to you

Does anybody owe you money? Yes/No

If yes, please give details of the debtor(s) and
amount(s)

	1	2	3
Debtor			
Amount			

4. Liabilities

Please give details of money you owe, for example:

4.1 Credit card debts

	1	2	3
Name and address			
of lender			
Amount owed			
Monthly instalment			

4.2 Hire purchase (please complete for each hire purchase arrangement you have)

	1	2	3
Name and address			
of lender			
Amount owed			
Monthly instalment			

4.3 Finance on vehicles (please complete for each vehicle subject to finance)

	1	2	3
Name and address of lender			
Amount owed			
Monthly instalment			

4.4 Catalogue debts (please complete for each debt)

	1	2	3
Lender			
Amount owed			
Weekly/monthly instalment			

4.5 County Court judgments (please complete for each judgment)

	1	2	3
Creditor			
Amount owed			
Monthly instalment			

4.6 Bank loans (but excluding any mortgage previously mentioned) (please complete for each loan)

	1	2	3
Lender			
Amount owed			
Monthly instalment			

4.7 Any other debts (please complete for each debt)

	1	2	3
Lender			
Amount owed			
Weekly/monthly instalment			

5. Monthly income and expenditure

A Income

Wages or salary after tax and NI   £____ per week/month

Pension   £____ per week/month

Other income   £____ per week/month

Partner's net wages or salary £____ per week/month

Child benefit   £____   per week/month

State income (please specify)   £____   per week/month

Maintenance   £____   per week/month

Other (please specify)   £____   per week/month

£____ per week/month

£____ per week/month

B Expenditure

Mortgage or rent   £____   per week/month

Gas/electricity   £____   per week/month

Telephone   £____   per week/month

Insurances (please specify)   £____   per week/month

Pension contributions   £____   per week/month

Travel (public transport)   £____   per week/month

Car expenses   £____   per week/month

Food   £____   per week/month

Council tax   £____   per week/month

Water rates £____ per week/month

Other (please specify)   £____   per
week/month

£____ per week/month

£____ per week/month

Total expenditure   £____   per week/month

C Other Payment

Add up any weekly/monthly instalments from
section 4 and enter the total here   £____   per
week/month

Disposable income

Income   £____   per week/month

less

Expenditure (B+C) £____   per week/month

Balance   £____   per week/month

I confiirm this is an accurate record of my/our
finanical affairs at [date].

Signed _____

Application for charging order nisi

This application assumes that the debtor is the sole owner of the property which is the subject of the application. If the debtor is co-owner of the property, you are still entitled to a charging order over the debtor's share, but you may not be able to obtain an order for the property to be sold – because the court will take into account the rights of the other owner. Take professional advice.

We also assume that the property is registered at HM Land Registry, and is subject to an existing mortgage, as this is the commonest situation. You can claim interest only if the judgment debt is for more than £5000 or the right to interest arises under the Late Payment of Commercial Debts (Interest) Act 1998.

In the [   ] County Court
Claim No. [   ]

In the Matter of the Charging Orders Act 1979 and In the Matter of [insert address of property] ('the property')

BETWEEN   Claimant

AND   Defendant

TAKE NOTICE that the claimant applies *ex parte* for an order that the defendant's beneficial interest in the property should be charged with:

- payment of [£   ] which is the unpaid balance of the judgment debt due and payable under an order dated [date]
- interest on the judgment debt, if allowable
- the costs of this application

Dated this [   ] day of [   ] [year]

Signature of claimant

Affidavit in support of application for charging order nisi

In the [_____] County Court

Claim No. [_____]

In the Matter of the Charging Orders Act 1979

and In the Matter of [insert address of property] ('the property')

BETWEEN   Claimant

AND   Defendant

Claimant's Affidavit

I [name] of [address]

make oath and say:

1. I am the claimant, and I am making my affadavit in support of my application for a charging order nisi over the defendant's property at [address] ('the property').

2. The defendant is [name] of [address]

3. On [date], I obtained judgment against the defendant for the sum of

[£   ]. The judgment debt was payable forthwith, and the balance outstanding is [£   ].

OR The judgment debt was payable by instalments, and the unpaid instalments amount to [£   ].

4. The defendant is the registered proprietor and beneficial owner of the property, which is registered at HM Land Registry under Title No [_____]. An office copy of the register maintained at HM Land Registry for the property is attached as an exhibit to this affidavit.

5.* I am aware that the defendant has the following creditors:

[details of mortgage lender, if there is one]

[other creditors, if you know of any]

6. The facts stated in this affidavit are within my knowledge, and I believe them to be true. I ask the court to grant my application.

SWORN at

on

before me

Solicitor/Court Official

Note: On the office copy of the Land Registry entry, you need to write:

'This is the exhibit referred to in the affidavit of [your name], sworn before me [name of solicitor or official] on [date].'

* If you are not aware of any mortgage on the property or any other creditors. State 'None known to me'.

Note: If the charge is over something other than real estate, such as shares, you must also state on the affidavit the name and address of the company, and you should send them a copy of your charging order nisi when you receive it.

Affidavit of service

This is the affidavit of service which you need to show that you have served the charging order nisi on your debtor. Note that you should serve an original of the order which has the court's seal on it, and not a photocopy.

In the [   ] County Court

Claim No. [   ]

BETWEEN
Claimant

AND
Defendant

Affidavit of service

I   make oath and say as follows:

1.   The Court made a charging order nisi in this matter on [   ], ('the charging order nisi'), a copy of which is attached as an exhibit to this affidavit.

2.   On [date] I sent an original of the charging order nisi, sealed by the court, by first class prepaid post to the defendant at

        [address].

3.   The Royal Mail has not returned as undelivered the envelope in which the charging order nisi was sent.

SWORN BY

at

in the County of

this day of

before me

Solicitor/Commissioner for Oaths

Endorse on the copy of the charging order nisi which accompanies your affidavit of service the following words:

This is the exhibit referred to in the affidavit of [your name] sworn before me: [name of solicitor or official on [date].

Worked example of creditor's bankruptcy petition (Form 6.7)

Form 6.7 is the bankruptcy petition to use where the debtor has failed to comply with a statutory demand for a debt payable immediately. This is by far the most common situation, but there are other situations and other forms to cover them. Apply to a law stationer and/or take professional advice if you think this may apply to you.

The marginal notes on the form are mostly straightforward, but we have given a few points overleaf which you may find helpful.

- Only fill in 'and lately residing at/lately carrying on business as' if the debtor has recently changed address or occupation.

- In clause 4 you must say *how* the statutory demand was served (eg by personal service) and *when* it was served – before or after 1700 on Monday to Friday, or any time on Saturday or Sunday.

- Ignore note (m) unless for some reason you are petitioning for bankruptcy before the three-week period from service of the statutory demand has elapsed.

- Leave the Endorsement blank for the court to give the hearing date.

You need this book first

<table>
<tr><td>

FORM 6.7

Rule 6 6 Creditor s Bankruptcy
Petition on Failure to Comply
with a Statutory Demand for a
Liquidated Sum Payable
Immediately

</td><td>

In the[†]

IN BANKRUPTCY

</td><td>

No.   **of**

</td></tr>
</table>

† Enter "High Court of Justice
or _____County Court' as
the case may be

‡ Insert full name of Debtor
(if known)

RE ‡ William Sykes

(a) Insert full name(s) and address(es) of petitioner(s)

I/We[(a)] John Henry Brownlow
27 Dickens Street
LONDON WC290T

(b) Insert full name place of residence and occupation (if any) of debtor

petition the court that a bankruptcy order may be made against [(b)]

William Sykes
Fagin's Yard, Lowlife Street, London EL1 5ZD
                                    Antique dealer

(c) Insert in full any other name(s) by which the debtor is or has been known

[also known as [(c)]

Bill Sikes

(d) Insert trading name (adding with another or others if this is so) business address and nature of business

[and carrying on business as [(d)]

Bill's Bric à Brac
14 Oliver Arcade
London WI9 1YF, Antique dealer

(e) Insert any other address or addresses at which the debtor has resided at or after the time the petition debt was incurred

[and lately residing at [(e)]

(f) Give the same details as specified in note (d) above for any other businesses which have been carried on at or after the time the petition debt was incurred

[and lately carrying on business as [(f)]

and say as follows

1   The debtor has for the greater part of six months immediately preceding the presentation of this petition [(g)] [resided at] [carried on business at]

(g) Delete as applicable

(h) Or as the case may be following the terms of Rule 6 9

Fagin's Yard, Lowlife Street, London EL15CD
within the district of this court[(h)]

(j) Please give the amount of debt(s) what they relate to and when they were incurred Please show separately the amount or rate of any interest or other charge not previously notified to the debtor and the reasons why you are claiming it

2   The debtor is justly and truly indebted to me[us] in the aggregate sum of £[(j)] 4,000 00
under an invoice dated 31 August 1999
for the sale of climbing equipment

3   The above-mentioned debt is for a liquidated sum payable immediately and the debtor appears to be unable to pay it

TSO 12

118

(k) Insert date of service of a statutory demand

4 On ⁱ *8 January 2 000*

a statutory demand was served upon the debtor by

(l) State manner of service of demand

ⁱ *personal service before 1700 hours*

in respect of the above mentioned debt To the best of my knowledge and belief the

demand has neither been complied with nor set aside in accordance with the Rules and no

application to set it aside is outstanding

(m) If 3 weeks have not elapsed since service of statutory demand give reasons for earlier presentation of petition

ᵐ

5 I/We do not nor does any person on my/our behalf hold any security on the debtor s

estate or any part thereof for the payment of the above mentioned sum OR

(n) Delete as applicable

I/We hold security for the payment of ⁿ [part of] of the above mentioned sum

I/We will give up such security for the benefit of all the creditors in the event of a

bankruptcy order being made OR

I/We hold security for the payment of part of the above mentioned sum and I/we estimate

the value of such security to be £

This petition is not made in respect of the secured part of my/our debt

---

Endorsement

This petition having been presented to the court on

it is ordered that the petition shall be heard as follows

Date

Time   hours

Place

(p) Insert name of debtor

and you the above named ᵖ   are to take

notice that if you intend to oppose the petition you must not later than 7 days before

the day fixed for the hearing

    (i) file in court a notice (in Form 6 19) specifying the grounds on which you object

       to the making of a bankruptcy order and

    (ii) send a copy of the notice to the petitioner or his solicitor

(q) Only to be completed where the petitioning creditor is represented by a solicitor

The solicitor to the petitioning creditor is ᵠ

Name

Address

Telephone Number

Reference

TSO 12

119

Worked example of winding-up petition (Form 4.2)

Creditors' winding-up petitions where the creditor is not represented by a solicitor are uncommon. Few courts stock the forms and at the time of going to press these were not available on line. Too much is at stake to risk getting your paperwork wrong. Get it checked by a court official, who will know how their own district judge likes things presented.

Note that the information required about the debtor company is freely available over the telephone from Companies House (see *Useful Contacts*).

The Endorsement is left blank for the court to set the hearing date.

Winding up
Petition
No 4.2 (Rule 4.7)

IN THE Bronte **No**   **of**
County Court

(1) Insert name
of Company

IN THE MATTER of (¹) Moorland Constructions Ltd

AND

IN THE MATTER of the Insolvency Act 1986

2 Insert title of
Court

To (²) the Bronte County Court

(3) Insert full name(s)
and address(es)
of Petitioner(s)

The Petition of (³) Heathcliff Enterprises Limited
of Wuthering Heights, Haworth, Yorkshire
BD17 2EB

(4) Insert date of
incorporation

1 Moorland Construction   Limited ( )
(hereinafter called "the Company") was incorporated on (⁴) 1 July 1997
under the Companies Act 19

(5) Insert address of
registered office

2 The registered office of the Company is at (⁵)
Earnshaw Mill, Oakworth, Yorkshire BD14 9HE

3 The nominal capital of the Company is £100·00   divided into
100 shares of £1·00   each The amount of the capital paid up or
credited as paid up is £100 00

4 The principal objects for which the Company was established are as follows

The construction and maintenance
of theme parks

and other objects stated in the Memorandum of Association of the
Company

(6) Set out the
grounds
on which a
Winding up
Order is sought

5 (⁶) on (date) a statutory demand was
served by the petitioner at the

[P T O

TSO 16

121

registered office of the company
The said statutory demand required
the company to pay the sum of
£15,000, of which particulars are
as follows

The debt arises under a contract
dated (date) by which the
petitioner agreed to supply the
company with roller coaster
equipment at a price of £15,000

As at the date of the statutory
demand the entire sum of
£15,000 was due and unpaid

Note   This margin is reserved for binding and must net be written across

6   In the circumstances it is just and equitable that the Company
    should be wound up

    Your Petitioner therefore prays as follows

    (1)That( ) Moorland Construction
    Limited may be wound up by the Court under the provisions of
    the Insolvency Act 1986 or

    (2)That such other Order may be made as the Court thinks fit

Note   (') It is intended to serve this Petition on the Company

7 f the Company
s Pet t oner de ete
note and add the
wo da   t s not
ntended to se ve
th s Pet t on upon
any person   Add
the full name and
add ess of any
othe person on
whom t s ntended
to serve he
Pet t on

[P T O

TSO 18

123

You need this book first

Endorsement

This Petition having been presented to the court

on   will be heard at (a) [Royal Courts of Justice

Strand London WC2A 2LL] [(b)   The Bronte   County Court]

[(c)   District Registry   ]

on

Date

Time   hours
(or as soon thereafter as the Petition can be heard)

~~The solicitor to the Petitioner is~~

Name

Address

Telephone No

Reference

(a) [Whose London Agents are

Name

Address

Telephone No

Reference   ]

a Delete as appl cab e

b) Inse t name and address of Court

(c) Inse t name and address of D str ct Reg stry

TSO 6

Advertisement of winding-up petition

This wording should accompany Form 4.2 when you apply to advertise in the *London Gazette*.

Advertisement of winding-up petition

[Insolvency, Companies, Winding-up]

A Petition to wind up the above-named Company of

[registered office] presented on
  by   of

[name and address of petitioner] claiming to be
[creditor] [contributory]

of the Company will be heard at
                     County Court

at

Date

Time   hours (or as soon thereafter as the Petition can be heard)

Any person intending to appear on the hearing of the Petition (whether to support or oppose it) must give notice of intention to do so to the Petitioner or [his]

[its] solicitor in accordance with Rule 4.16 by 16.00 hours on _____[a business day before the hearing date]

DATED_____

Certificate of compliance (liquidation)

You will need to file this certificate with the court at least five days before the hearing date, together with a cutting from the *London Gazette* showing your advertisement.

Certificate of compliance

[Insolvency, Companies, Service]

Winding-up Petition on

I certify that the above-mentioned Petition which will be heard on

was served in accordance with the provisions of Rule 4.11 on   and was advertised in accordance with the provisions of Rule 4.11 on in the *London Gazette* on

DATED

SIGNED

NOTE: A copy of the advertisement must be filed in court with this certificate.

Official forms

You may make multiple copies of the following court forms, or you may use the top copy directly to fill in your details. You may access many of these forms from the Court Service's website (http://www.courtservice.gov.uk).

A summary of the forms is as follows:

Page 130   Claim form (N1)

Page 134   Certificate of service (N215)

Page 136   Request for oral examination (N316)

Page 137   Request for warrant of execution (N323)

Page 138   Request for reissue of warrant (N445)

Page 139   Request for attachment of earnings order (N337)

Page 140   Request for reissue of enforcement or oral examination (N446)

Page 141   Affidavit in support of application for garnishee order absolute (N349)

Page 142   Statutory demand (Insolvency-Bankruptcy 6.1)

Page 146   Statutory demand (Insolvency-Bankruptcy 6.2)

Page 150   Affidavit of personal service of statutory demand (Insolvency-Bankruptcy 6.11)

Page 151   Creditors bankruptcy petition (Insolvency-Bankruptcy 6.7)

Page 153   Affidavit of truth of statements in bankruptcy petition (Insolvency-Bankruptcy 6.13)

Page 154   Affidavit of personal service of bankruptcy petition (Insolvency-Bankruptcy 6.17)

Page 155   Statutory demand (Insolvency-Company 4.1)

Page 159   Winding-up petition (Insolvency - company 4.2)

Page 163   Affidavit verifying winding-up petition (Insolvency – Company 4.3)

Page 165   Affidavit of service of winding-up petition at registered office (Insolvency – Company 4.4)

Page 167   Affidavit of service of winding-up petition other than at registered office or an oversea company (Insolvency – Company 4.5)

Page 168   Application for a fee exemption or remission (EX160)

You need this book first

Claim Form (N1)

	Claim Form	In the	
		Claim No.	

Claimant

(SEAL)

Defendant(s)

Brief details of claim

Value

Defendant's name and address		£
	Amount claimed	
	Court fee	
	Solicitor's costs	
	Total amount	
	Issue date	

The court office at

is open between 10am and 4pm Monday to Friday. When corresponding with the court, please address forms or letters to the Court Manager and quote the claim number.

N1 Claim Form (CPR Part 7) (4.99)

TSO 1 N1: 1 of 4

Claim No.	

Does, or will, your claim include any issues under
the Human Rights Act 1998? ☐ Yes ☐ No

Particulars of Claim (attached) (to follow)

Statement of Truth
* (I believe)(The Claimant believes) that the facts stated in these particulars of claim are true.
* I am duly authorised by the claimant to sign this statement

Full name

Name of claimant's solicitor's firm

signed _____ position or office held _____

* (Claimant)(Litigation friend)(Claimant's solicitor) (if signing on behalf of firm or company)
* *delete as appropriate*

Claimant's or claimant's solicitor's address to
which documents or payments should be sent if
different from overleaf including (if appropriate)
details of DX, fax or e-mail.

TSO 1 N1: 2 of 4

You need this book first

Notes for claimant on completing a claim form

Further information may be obtained from the court in a series of free leaflets.

- Please read all of these guidance notes before you begin completing the claim form. The notes follow the order in which information is required on the form.
- Court staff can help you fill in the claim form and give information about procedure once it has been issued. But they cannot give legal advice. If you need legal advice, for example, about the likely success of your claim or the evidence you need to prove it, you should contact a solicitor or a Citizens Advice Bureau.
- If you are filling in the claim form by hand, please use black ink and write in block capitals.
- Copy the completed claim form and the defendant's notes for guidance so that you have one copy for yourself, one copy for the court and one copy for each defendant. Send or take the forms to the court office with the appropriate fee. The court will tell you how much this is.

Notes on completing the claim form

Heading

You must fill in the heading of the form to indicate whether you want the claim to be issued in a county court or in the High Court (The High Court means either a District Registry (attached to a county court) or the Royal Courts of Justice in London). There are restrictions on claims which may be issued in the High Court (see 'Value' overleaf).

Use whichever of the following is appropriate:

'In the.................................County Court'
(inserting the name of the court)

or

'In the High Court of Justice.........................Division'
(inserting e.g. 'Queen's Bench' or 'Chancery' as appropriate)
'...District Registry'
(inserting the name of the District Registry)

or

'In the High Court of Justice.........................Division,
(inserting e.g. 'Queen's Bench' or 'Chancery' as appropriate)
Royal Courts of Justice'

Claimant and defendant details

As the person issuing the claim, you are called the 'claimant'; the person you are suing is called the 'defendant'. Claimants who are under 18 years old (unless otherwise permitted by the court) and patients within the meaning of the Mental Health Act 1983, must have a litigation friend to issue and conduct court proceedings on their behalf. Court staff will tell you more about what you need to do if this applies to you.

You must provide the following information about yourself **and** the defendant according to the capacity in which you are suing and in which the defendant is being sued.

When suing or being sued as:-

an individual:

All known forenames and surname, whether Mr, Mrs, Miss, Ms or Other (e.g. Dr) and residential address (**including** postcode and telephone number) in England and Wales. Where the defendant is a proprietor of a business, a partner in a firm or an individual sued in the name of a club or other unincorporated association, the address for service should be the usual or last known place of residence **or** principal place of business of the company, firm or club or other unincorporated association.

Where the individual is:

under 18 write '(a child by Mr Joe Bloggs his litigation friend)' after the name. If the child is conducting proceedings on their own behalf write '(a child)' after the child's name.

a patient within the meaning of the Mental Health Act 1983 write '(by Mr Joe Bloggs his litigation friend)' after the patient's name.

trading under another name

you must add the words 'trading as' and the trading name e.g. 'Mr John Smith trading as Smith's Groceries'.

suing or being sued in a representative capacity

you must say what the capacity is e.g. 'Mr Joe Bloggs as the representative of Mrs Sharon Bloggs (deceased)'.

suing or being sued in the name of a club or other unincorporated association

add the words 'suing/sued on behalf of' followed by the name of the club or other unincorporated association.

a firm

enter the name of the firm followed by the words 'a firm' e.g. 'Bandbox - a firm' and an address for service which is either a partner's residential address or the principal or last known place of business.

a corporation (other than a company)

enter the full name of the corporation and the address which is either its principal office **or** any other place where the corporation carries on activities and which has a real connection with the claim.

a company registered in England and Wales

enter the name of the company and an address which is either the company registered office **or** any place of business that has a real, or the most, connection with the claim e.g. the shop where the goods were bought.

an overseas company (defined by s744 of the Companies Act 1985)

enter the name of the company and either the address registered under s691 of the Act **or** the address of the place of business having a real, or the most, connection with the claim.

N1A Notes for claimant (4.99) Printed on behalf of the Crown Service

Brief details of claim

Note: the facts and full details about your claim and whether or not you are claiming interest, should be set out in the 'particulars of claim' *(see note under 'Particulars of Claim').*

You must set out under **this** heading:

- a concise statement of the nature of your claim
- the remedy you are seeking e.g. payment of money; an order for return of goods or their value; an order to prevent a person doing an act; damages for personal injuries.

Value

If you are claiming a **fixed amount of money** (a 'specified amount') write the amount in the box at the bottom right-hand corner of the claim form against 'amount claimed'.

If you are not claiming a fixed amount of money (an 'unspecified amount') under 'Value' write "I expect to recover" followed by whichever of the following applies to your claim:

- "not more than £5,000" **or**
- "more than £5,000 but not more than £15,000" **or**
- "more than £15,000"

If you are **not able** to put a value on your claim, write " I cannot say how much I expect to recover".

Personal injuries

If your claim is for 'not more than £5,000' and includes a claim for personal injuries, you must also write "My claim includes a claim for personal injuries and the amount I expect to recover as damages for pain, suffering and loss of amenity is" followed by either:

- "not more than £1,000" **or**
- "more than £1,000"

Housing disrepair

If your claim is for 'not more than £5,000' and includes a claim for housing disrepair relating to residential premises, you must also write "My claim includes a claim against my landlord for housing disrepair relating to residential premises. The cost of the repairs or other work is estimated to be" followed by either:

- "not more than £1,000" **or**
- "more than £1,000"

If within this claim, you are making a claim for other damages, you must also write:

"I expect to recover as damages" followed by either :

- "not more than £1,000" **or**
- "more than £1,000"

Issuing in the High Court

You may only issue in the High Court if one of the following statements applies to your claim:-

"By law, my claim must be issued in the High Court. The Act which provides this is.................(specify Act)"

or

"I expect to recover more than £15,000"

or

"My claim includes a claim for personal injuries and the value of the claim is £50,000 or more"

or

"My claim needs to be in a specialist High Court list, namely................................(state which list)".

If one of the statements does apply and you wish to, or must by law, issue your claim in the High Court, write the words "I wish my claim to issue in the High Court because" followed by the relevant statement e.g. "I wish my claim to issue in the High Court because my claim includes a claim for personal injuries and the value of my claim is £50,000 or more."

Defendant's name and address

Enter in this box the full names and addresses of the defendants receiving the claim form (ie. one claim form for each defendant). If the defendant is to be served outside England and Wales, you may need to obtain the court's permission.

Particulars of claim

You may include your particulars of claim on the claim form in the space provided or in a separate document which you should head 'Particulars of Claim'. It should include the names of the parties, the court, the claim number and your address for service and also contain a statement of truth. You should keep a copy for yourself, provide one for the court and one for each defendant. Separate particulars of claim can either be served:

- with the claim form **or**
- within 14 days after the date on which the claim form was served.

If your particulars of claim are served separately from the claim form, they must be served with the forms on which the defendant may reply to your claim.

Your particulars of claim must include

- a concise statement of the facts on which you rely
- a statement (if applicable) to the effect that you are seeking aggravated damages or exemplary damages
- details of any interest which you are claiming
- any other matters required for your type of claim as set out in the relevant practice direction.

Address for documents

Insert in this box the address at which you wish to receive documents and/or payments, if different from the address you have already given under the heading 'Claimant'. The address must be in England or Wales.

If you are willing to accept service by DX, fax or e-mail, add details.

Statement of truth

This must be signed by you, by your solicitor or your litigation friend, as appropriate.

Where the claimant is a registered company or a corporation the claim must be signed by either the director, treasurer, secretary, chief executive, manager or other officer of the company or (in the case of a corporation) the mayor, chairman, president or town clerk.

You need this book first

Certificate of Service (N215)

Certificate of Service

In the	
Claim No.	
Claimant	
Defendant	

On the *(insert date)*

the *(insert title or description of documents served)*

a copy of which is attached to this notice was served on *(insert name of person served, including position i.e. partner, director if appropriate)*

Tick as appropriate

☐ by first class post

☐ by Document Exchange

☐ by delivering to or leaving

☐ by handing it to or leaving it with

☐ by fax machine (time sent)
(you may want to enclose a copy of the transmission sheet)

☐ by e-mail

☐ by other means *(please specify)*

at *(insert address where service effected, include fax or DX number or e-mail address)*

being the defendant's:

☐ residence

☐ registered office

☐ place of business

☐ other *(please specify)*

The date of service is therefore deemed to be *(insert date – see over for guidance)*

I confirm that at the time of signing this Certificate the document has not been returned to me as undelivered.

Signed
(Claimant)(Defendant)('s Solicitor)('s Litigation friend)

Position or office held
(if signing on behalf of firm or company)

Date

TSO 2 N215: 1 of 2

Notes for guidance

Please note that these notes are only a guide and are not exhaustive.

Where to serve If you are in doubt you should refer to Part 6 of the rules.

Nature of party to be served	Place of service
Individual	• usual or last known residence
Proprietor of business	• usual or last known residence; or • place of business or last known place of business
Individual who is suing or being sued in the name of a firm	• usual or last known residence; or • principal or last known place of business of the firm
Corporation (incorporated in England and Wales) other than a company	• principal office of the corporation; or • any place of business within the jurisdiction where the corporation carries on its activities and which has a real connection with the claim
Company registered in England and Wales	• principal office of the company or corporation; or • any place of business of the company within the jurisdiction which has a real connection with the claim

Personal Service A document is served personally on an individual by leaving it with that individual. A document is served personally on a company or other corporation by leaving it with a person holding a senior position within the company or corporation. In the case of a partnership, you must leave it with either a partner or a person having control or management at the principal place of business. Where a solicitor is authorised to accept service on behalf of a party, service must be effected on the solicitor, unless otherwise ordered.

Deemed Service Part 6.7(1). A document which is served in accordance with these rules or any relevant practice direction shall be deemed to be served on the day shown in the following table.

Method of service	Deemed day of service
First class post	The second day after it was posted
Document exchange	The second day after it was left at the document exchange
Delivering the document to or leaving it at a permitted address	The day after it was delivered to or left at the permitted address
Fax	If it is transmitted on a business day before 4pm., on that day, or otherwise on the business day after the day on which it was transmitted.
Other electronic method	The second day after the day on which it was transmitted.

• If a document (other than a claim form) is served after 5pm on a business day, or at any time on a Saturday, Sunday or a bank holiday, the document shall, for the purpose of calculating any period of time after service of the document, be treated as having been served on the next business day.

• In this context "business day" means any day except Saturday, Sunday or a bank holiday; and "bank holiday" includes Christmas Day and Good Friday.

Service of documents on children and patients – The rules relating to service on children and patients are contained in Part 6.6 of the rules.

Claim Forms – The general rules about service are subject to the special rules about service of claim forms contained in rules 6.12 to 6.16.

TSO 2 N215: 2 of 2

Request for Oral Examination

to be completed and signed by the claimant or his solicitor and sent to the court with the appropriate fee

1 Claimant's name and address

In the

County Court

Claim Number

2 Name and address for service and payment
(if different from above)
Ref/Tel No.

For court use only

O/E no.

Issue date:

3 Defendant's name and address

Hearing date:

on

at   o'clock

4 Name and address of person to be orally examined if different from Box 3
(ie director of defendant company)

at (address)

5 Judgment details

Court where judgment order made if not court of issue

I apply for an order that the above defendant (the officer of the defendant company name in Box 4) attend and be orally examined as to his (the defendant company's) financial circumstances and produce at the examination any relevant books or documents.

6 Outstanding debt

* you may be able to claim interest if judgment is entered for £5,000 or more, or is in respect of a debt which attracts contractual or statutory interest for late payment

Balance of debt and any interest*/damages at date of this request

Issue fee

AMOUNT NOW DUE

Unsatisfied warrant costs

I certify that the balance now due is as shown

Signed

Claimant (Claimant's solicitor)

Date

IMPORTANT
You must inform the court immediately of any payments you receive after you have sent this request to the court

N316 Request for oral examination (4.99)
© Crown copyright. Reproduced by The Stationery Office. *Printed on behalf of The Court Service*

TSO 3 N316: 1 of 1

Request for Warrant of Execution

to be completed and signed by the claimant or his solicitor and sent to the court with the appropriate fee

1 Claimant's name and address		**In the**
		County Court
		Claim Number

2 Name and address for service and payment *(if different from above)* **Ref/Tel No.**		*For court use only*
		Warrant no.
		Issue date:
		Warrant applied for at o'clock
3 Defendant's name and address		Foreign court code/name:

4 Warrant details

(A) Balance due at date of this request ←

(B) Amount for which warrant to issue

Issue fee

Solicitor's costs

Land Registry fee

TOTAL

If the amount of the warrant at (B) is less than the balance at (A), the sum due after the warrant is paid will be

I certify that the whole or part of any instalments due under the judgment or order have not been paid and the balance now due is as shown

Signed

Claimant (Claimant's solicitor)

Date

IMPORTANT
You must inform the court immediately of any payments you receive after you have sent this request to the court

You should provide a contact number so that the bailiff can speak to you if he/she needs to:

Daytime phone number: Evening phone number (if possible):

Contact name (where appropriate):

Defendant's phone number (if known):

If you have any other information which may help the bailiff or if you have reason to believe that the bailiff may encounter difficulties you should write it below.

Warrant No.

N323 Request for warrant of execution (4.99)

1999 Edition 4.99

© Crown copyright. Reproduced by The Stationery Office.

TSO 4 N323, 1 of 1

You need this book first

Request for Reissue of Warrant (N445)

Request for Reissue of Warrant

tick appropriate box and enter case number and warrant number

In the

County Court

Claim Number

Warrant Number

Type of warrant		
	☐	**Warrant of execution**
	☐	**Warrant of possession**
	☐	**Warrant of delivery**
	☐	**Warrant of committal**

1 Claimant's name

2 Name and Address for Service and Payment

Ref/Tel No.

3 Defendant's Name and Address

I certify that the whole or part of any instalments due under the judgment or order have not been paid and the balance now due is as shown (*and that the amount due under the part warrant is as shown at (B)† and/or the defendant has not vacated the land as ordered)

4 Warrant details

(A) Balance of judgment or order due at date of this request including fee and costs of warrant issue and reissue, where appropriate. The reissue fee applies only to warrant of execution. (There is no fee to reissue a suspended warrant).

Signed

Claimant (Claimant's Solicitor)

(B) Part warrants only
Balance due under the warrant fee and costs of warrant issue and reissue, where appropriate. The reissue fee applies only to warrant of execution. (There is no fee to reissue a suspended warrant).

Date

* delete if not a part warrant
† delete if not a possession warrant

If the amount of the warrant at (B) is less than the balance at (A), the sum due after the warrant is paid will be

IMPORTANT

You must inform the court immediately of any payments you receive after you have sent this request to the court

Reasons for requesting reissue (information you are relying on to support your application for reissue e.g. address or execution has changed, failure to make payments under a suspended order etc. You should also tell the court if you have reason to believe that the bailiff might encounter any serious difficulty in attempting to execute the warrant.)

N445 Request for reissue of warrant (4/99) © Crown copyright. Reproduced by The Stationery Office.

TSO 5 N445: 1 of 1

Request for attachment of Earnings Order (N337)

Request for Attachment of Earnings Order

to be completed and signed by the claimant or his solicitor and sent to the court with the appropriate fee

1 **Claimant's name and address**

In the

County Court

Claim Number

2 **Name and address for service and payment** *(if different from above)* **Ref/Tel No.**

For court use only

A/E no.

Issue date:

Hearing date:

3 **Defendant's name and address**

on

at   o'clock

at (address)

4 **Judgment details**

Court where judgment order made if not court of issue

I apply for an attachment of earnings order

5 **Outstanding debt**

Balance due at date of request*
(excluding issue fee but including unsatisfied warrant costs)

* you may also be entitled to interest to date of request where judgment is for £5,000 or more, or is in respect of a debt which attracts contractual or statutory interest for late payment

Issue fee

AMOUNT NOW DUE

I certify that the whole or part of any instalments due under the judgment or order have not been paid and the balance now due is as shown

Signed

Claimant (Claimant's solicitor)

Date

6 **Employment Details** *(please give as much information as you can – it will help the court to make an order more quickly)*

Employer's name and address

7 **Other details**

(Give any other details about the defendant's circumstances which may be relevant to the application)

Defendant's place of work
(if different from employer's address)

The defendant is employed as

Works No/Pay Ref

IMPORTANT
You must inform the court immediately of any payments you receive after you have sent this request to the court

N337 Request for attachment of earnings order (4.99) © Crown copyright. Reproduced by The Stationery Office. *Printed on behalf of The Court Service*

TSO 6 N337: 1 of 1

You need this book first

Request for Reissue of Enforcement or Oral Examination (N446)

Request for Reissue of Enforcement or Oral Examination (not warrant)

In the

County Court

Claim No.

Type of Process			
(Tick appropriate box and enter claim number and number of process).		**Attachment of earnings**	A/E No.
		Oral examination	O/E No.
		Judgment summons	J/S No.
		Other *please specify, charging order, garnishee etc.*	No.

1 Claimant's name

2 Name and Address for Service and Payment

Ref/Tel No.

3 Defendant's Name and Address

For court use only

Hearing Date:

on

at   *o'clock*

at (address)

Reissue date:

---

4 Outstanding debt
(A) Balance due* at date of this request (including costs of issue of post-judgment process and unsatisfied warrant costs)†.

*This may include interest to the date of request where judgment is for £5,000 or more, or is in respect of a debt which attracts contractual or statutory interest for late payment.

† Except where reissuing oral examination

Unsatisfied warrant costs (oral examinations only)

(B) **Judgment summonses only**
Amount due under the judgment summons (do not include amounts for which Defendant imprisoned).

IMPORTANT
You must inform the court immediately of any payments you receive after you have sent this request to the court.

I certify that (*the whole or part of any instalments due under the judgment or order have not been paid and that) the balance now due under this judgment is as shown († and that the amount due under the judgment summons is as shown at (B)).

Signed

Claimant (Claimant's Solicitor)

Date

* delete if you are applying to reissue an oral examination.
† delete if not applying to reissue judgment summons.

Reasons for requesting reissue *(information you are relying on to support your application for reissue e.g. Defendant's address (or employment) has changed, he has failed to make payments under a suspended order etc.)*

Reissue No.

N446 Request for reissue of post-judgment process (other than warrant) (4.99) © Crown copyright. Reproduced by The Stationery Office.

TSO 7 N446: 1 of 1

140

Affidavit in support of Application for Garnishee Order Absolute (N349)

Affidavit in support of Application for Garnishee Order Absolute

Sworn by (deponent)	on (date)
This is the (1st, 2nd etc)	affidavit
filed on behalf of (party)	by this deponent
on (date filed)	

Claimant ——————————————————————

Defendant ——————————————————————

Garnishee ——————————————————————

In the

County Court

Claim No. *always quote this*	
Claimant's Ref.	

I, [Insert full name, address and occupation of deponent]

(Solicitor for) the above-named claimant, make oath and say:

1. That I (or)
   on the   day   [20   ], obtained a judgment (or an order) in this court against
   the above-named defendant for the payment of the sum of £   for
   debt (or damages) and costs

2. That £   , including any interest to date [where judgment is entered for more than
   £5000 or includes a sum in respect of contractual or late payment, the plaintiff may be entitled to further interest] is still due and unpaid
   under the judgment (order)

3. That to the best of my information or belief the garnishee,
   of

   is indebted to the defendant (in the sum of £   ) [add if known]
   The reasons for my information and belief are: [state your grounds]

4. That the garnishee is a deposit-taking institution having more than one place of business (and the name and address of the branch at
   which the defendant's account is believed to be held is:

   and the number of the account is believed to be   ) (I do not know at which
   branch the defendant's account is held, or what the number of the account is) [delete as appropriate]

5. That the last known address of the defendant is:

Sworn at in the	
of this	**Before me**
day of [20]	Officer of a court, appointed by the Circuit Judge to take affidavits

This affidavit is filed on behalf of the claimant

The court office at

is open between 10am and 4pm Monday to Friday. When corresponding with the court, please address forms and letters to the Court Manager and quote the claim number.

N349 Affidavit in support of application for garnishee order (Order 30, rule 2) (4.99)

Printed on behalf of The Court Service   © Crown copyright. Reproduced by The Stationery Office.

TSO B N349, 1 of 1

You need this book first

Statutory demand (Insolvency - Bankruptcy 6.1)

Form 6.1
Statutory Demand
under section 268(1)(a)
of the Insolvency
Act 1986.
Debt for Liquidated
Sum Payable
Immediately
(Rule 6.1)

WARNING

- This is an **important** document. You should refer to the notes entitled "How to comply with a Statutory Demand or have it set aside".

- If you wish to have this Demand set aside you must make application to do so **within 18 days** from its service on you.

- If you do not apply to set aside **within 18 days** or otherwise deal with this Demand as set out in the notes **within 21 days** after its service on you, you could be made bankrupt and your property and goods taken away from you.

- Please read the Demand and notes carefully. If you are in any doubt about your position you should seek advice **immediately** from a solicitor or your nearest Citizens Advice Bureau.

NOTES FOR CREDITOR
- If the Creditor is entitled to the debt by way of assignment, details of the original Creditor and any intermediary assignees should be given in part C on page 3.
- If the amount of debt includes interest not previously notified to the Debtor as included in the Debtor's liability, details should be given, including the grounds upon which interest is charged. The amount of interest must be shown separately.
- Any other charge accruing due from time to time may be claimed. The amount or rate of the charge must be identified and the grounds on which it is claimed must be stated.
- In either case the amount claimed must be limited to that which has accrued due at the date of the Demand.
- If the Creditor holds any security the amount of debt should be the sum the Creditor is prepared to regard as unsecured for the purposes of this Demand. Brief details of the total debt should be included and the nature of the security and the value put upon it by the Creditor, as at the date of the Demand, must be specified.
- If signatory of the Demand is a solicitor or other agent of the Creditor, the name of his/her firm should be given.

DEMAND

To
Address

This demand is served on you by the Creditor:
Name
Address

The Creditor claims that you owe the sum of £
full particulars of which are set out on page 2, and that it is payable immediately and, to the extent of the sum demanded, is unsecured.

The Creditor demands that you pay the above debt or secure or compound for it to the Creditor's satisfaction.

[The Creditor making this Demand is a Minister of the Crown or a Government Department, and it is intended to present a Bankruptcy Petition in the High Court in London.] [Delete if inappropriate].

Signature of individual

Name
(BLOCK LETTERS)

Date   day of

* Position with or relationship to Creditor:
* I am authorised to make this Demand on the Creditor's behalf.

Address

* Delete if signed by the Creditor himself.

Tel. No.   Ref. No.

N.B. The person making this Demand must complete the whole of pages 1, 2 and parts A, B and C (as applicable) on page 3.

[P.T.O

TSO 9 Insolvency – Bankruptcy 6.1: 1 of 4

Particulars of Debt
(These particulars must include (a) when the debt was incurred, (b) the consideration for the debt (or if there is no consideration the way in which it arose) and (c) the amount due as at the date of this demand).

NOTES FOR CREDITOR

● If the Creditor is entitled to the debt by way of assignment, details of the original Creditor and any intermediary assignees should be given in part C on page 3.

● If the amount of debt includes interest not previously notified to the Debtor as included in the Debtor's liability, details should be given, including the grounds upon which interest is charged. The amount of interest must be shown separately.

● Any other charge accruing due from time to time may be claimed. The amount or rate of the charge must be identified and the grounds on which it is claimed must be stated.

● In either case the amount claimed must be limited to that which has accrued due at the date of the demand.

● If the Creditor holds any security the amount of debt should be the sum the Creditor is prepared to regard as unsecured for the purposes of this Demand. Brief details of the total debt should be included and the nature of the security and the value put upon it by the Creditor, as at the date of the Demand, must be specified.

● If signatory is a solicitor or other agent of the Creditor, the name of his/her firm should be given.

NOTE
If space is insufficient continue on page 4 and clearly indicate on this page that you are doing so.

TSO 9 Insolvency – Bankruptcy 6.1: 2 of 4

Part A
Appropriate Court for Setting Aside Demand

Rule 6.4(2) of the Insolvency Rules 1986 states that the appropriate Court is the Court to which you would have to present your own Bankruptcy Petition in accordance with Rule 6.40(1) and 6.40(2). In accordance with those rules on present information the appropriate Court is [the High Court of Justice] [County Court]
(address)

Any application by you to set aside this Demand should be made to that Court.

Part B

The individual or individuals to whom any communication regarding this Demand may be addressed is/are:

Name ....
(BLOCK LETTERS)

Address ....

....

....

Telephone Number ....

Reference ....

Part C
For completion if the Creditor is entitled to the debt by way of assignment.

	Name	Date(s) of Assignment
Original Creditor		
Assignees		

How to comply with a Statutory Demand or have it set aside (ACT WITHIN 18 DAYS)

If you wish to avoid a Bankruptcy Petition being presented against you, you must pay the debt shown on page 1, particulars of which are set out on page 2 of this notice, within the period of **21 days** after its service upon you. Alternatively, you can attempt to come to a settlement with the Creditor. To do this you should:

- inform the individual (or one of the individuals) named in Part B above immediately that you are willing and able to offer security for the debt to the Creditor's satisfaction; *or*
- inform the individual (or one of the individuals) named in Part B above immediately that you are willing and able to compound for the debt to the Creditor's satisfaction.

If you dispute the Demand in whole or in part you should:

- contact the individual (or one of the individuals) named in Part B immediately.

If you consider that you have grounds to have this Demand set aside or if you do not quickly receive a satisfactory written reply from the individual named in Part B whom you have contacted you should **apply within 18 days** from the date of service of this Demand on you to the appropriate Court shown in Part A above to have the Demand set aside.

Any application to set aside the Demand (Form 6.4 in Schedule 4 of the Insolvency Rules 1986) should be made within 18 days from the date of service upon you and be supported by an Affidavit (Form 6.5 in Schedule 4 to those Rules) stating the grounds on which the Demand should be set aside. The forms may be obtained from the appropriate Court when you attend to make the application.

Remember: From the date of service on you of this document:
(a) you have only **18 days** to apply to the Court to have the Demand set aside, and
(b) you have only **21 days** before the Creditor may present a Bankruptcy Petition.

You need this book first

Statutory demand (Insolvency - Bankruptcy 6.2)

Form 6.2
Statutory Demand
under section 268(1)(a)
of the Insolvency
Act 1986.
Debt for Liquidated
Sum Payable
Immediately
Following a Judgment
or Order of the Court
(Rule 6.7)

WARNING

- This is an **important** document. You should refer to the notes entitled "How to comply with a Statutory Demand or have it set aside".

- If you wish to have this Demand set aside you must make application to do so **within 18 days** from its service on you.

- If you do not apply to set aside **within 18 days** or otherwise deal with this Demand as set out in the notes **within 21 days** after its service on you, you could be made bankrupt and your property and goods taken away from you.

- Please read the Demand and notes carefully. If you are in any doubt about your position you should seek advice **immediately** from a solicitor or your nearest Citizens Advice Bureau.

NOTES FOR CREDITOR

- If the Creditor is entitled to the debt by way of assignment, details of the original Creditor and any intermediary assignees should be given in part C on page 3.

- If the amount of debt includes interest not previously notified to the Debtor as included in the Debtor's liability, details should be given, including the grounds upon which interest is charged. The amount of interest must be shown separately.

- Any other charge accruing due from time to time may be claimed. The amount or rate of the charge must be identified and the grounds on which it is claimed must be stated.

- In either case the amount claimed must be limited to that which has accrued due at the date of the demand.

- If the Creditor holds any security the amount of debt should be the sum the Creditor is prepared to regard as unsecured for the purposes of this Demand. Brief details of the total debt should be included and the nature of the security and the value put upon it by the Creditor, as at the date of the Demand, must be specified.

- Details of the judgment or order should be inserted, including details of the Division of the Court or District Registry and Court reference, where judgment is obtained in the High Court.

- If signatory of the Demand is a solicitor or other agent of the Creditor, the name of his/her firm should be given.

* Delete if signed by the Creditor himself.

DEMAND

To
Address

This demand is served on you by the Creditor:
Name
Address

The Creditor claims that you owe the sum of £   ,
full particulars of which are set out on page 2, and that it is payable immediately and, to the extent of the sum demanded, is unsecured.

By a Judgment/Order of the High Court   /
                                                County Court proceedings entitled

(Case) Number   between
                                                            Plaintiff
and   Defendant
it was adjudged/ordered that you pay to the Creditor the sum of £
and £   for costs.

The Creditor demands that you pay the above debt or secure or compound for it to the Creditor's satisfaction.

[The Creditor making this Demand is a Minister of the Crown or a Government Department, and it is intended to present a Bankruptcy Petition in the High Court in London.] [Delete if inappropriate].

Signature of individual

Name
(BLOCK LETTERS)

Date   day of

* Position with or relationship to Creditor:
* I am authorised to make this Demand on the Creditor's behalf.
Address

Tel. No.   Ref. No.

N.B. The person making this Demand must complete the whole of pages 1, 2 and parts A, B and C (as applicable) on page 3.

[P.T.O

Particulars of Debt
(These particulars must include (a) when the debt was incurred, (b) the consideration for the debt (or if there is no consideration the way in which it arose) and (c) the amount due as at the date of this demand).

NOTES FOR CREDITOR

● If the Creditor is entitled to the debt by way of assignment, details of the original Creditor and any intermediary assignees should be given in part C on page 3.

● If the amount of debt includes interest not previously notified to the Debtor as included in the Debtor's liability, details should be given, including the grounds upon which interest is charged. The amount of interest must be shown separately.

● Any other charge accruing due from time to time may be claimed. The amount or rate of the charge must be identified and the grounds on which it is claimed must be stated.

● In either case the amount claimed must be limited to that which has accrued due at the date of the demand.

● If the Creditor holds any security the amount of debt should be the sum the Creditor is prepared to regard as unsecured for the purposes of this Demand. Brief details of the total debt should be included and the nature of the security and the value put upon it by the Creditor, as at the date of the Demand, must be specified.

● If signatory is a solicitor or other agent of the Creditor, the name of his/her firm should be given.

Note
If space is insufficient continue on page 4 and clearly indicate on this page that you are doing so.

You need this book first

Part A
Appropriate Court for Setting Aside Demand

Rule 6.4(2) of the Insolvency Rules 1986 states that the appropriate Court is the Court to which you would have to present your own Bankruptcy Petition in accordance with Rule 6.40(1) and 6.40(2).

Any application by you to set aside this Demand should be made to that Court, or, if this Demand is issued by a Minister of the Crown or a Government Department, you must apply to the High Court to set aside if it is intended to present a Bankruptcy Petition against you in the High Court (see page 1).

In accordance with those rules on present information the appropriate Court is [the High Court of Justice] [County Court] (address)

Part B
The individual or individuals to whom any communication regarding this Demand may be addressed is/are:

Name ....

(BLOCK LETTERS)

Address ....

....

....

Telephone Number ....

Reference ....

Part C
For completion if the Creditor is entitled to the debt by way of assignment.

	Name	Date(s) of Assignment
Original Creditor		
Assignees		

How to comply with a Statutory Demand or have it set aside (ACT WITHIN 18 DAYS)

If you wish to avoid a Bankruptcy Petition being presented against you, you must pay the debt shown on page 1, particulars of which are set out on page 2 of this notice, within the period of **21 days** after its service upon you. However, if the Demand follows (includes) a Judgment or Order of a County Court, any payment must be made to that County Court (quoting the Case No.). Alternatively, you can attempt to come to a settlement with the Creditor. To do this you should:

- inform the individual (or one of the individuals) named in Part B above immediately that you are willing and able to offer security for the debt to the Creditor's satisfaction; or

- inform the individual (or one of the individuals) named in Part B above immediately that you are willing and able to compound for the debt to the Creditor's satisfaction.

If you dispute the Demand in whole or in part you should:

- contact the individual (or one of the individuals) named in Part B immediately.

If you consider that you have grounds to have this Demand set aside or if you do not quickly receive a satisfactory written reply from the individual named in Part B whom you have contacted you should **apply within 18 days** from the date of service of this Demand on you to the appropriate Court shown in Part A above to have the Demand set aside.

Any application to set aside the Demand (Form 6.4 in Schedule 4 of the Insolvency Rules 1986) should be made within 18 days from the date of service upon you and be supported by an Affidavit (Form 6.5 in Schedule 4 to those Rules) stating the grounds on which the Demand should be set aside. The forms may be obtained from the appropriate Court when you attend to make the application.

Remember: From the date of service on you of this document:
(a) you have only **18 days** to apply to the Court to have the Demand set aside, and
(b) you have only **21 days** before the Creditor may present a Bankruptcy Petition.

You need this book first

Affidavit of personal service of statutory demand (Insolvency - Bankruptcy 6.11)

Form 6.11

Affidavit of Personal
Service of Statutory
Demand
(Rule 6.11)

*Enter High Court of
Justice *or* "_____
County Court" as
the case may be.

(1) Insert name,
address,
description
(occupation) of
person making
the Oath.

† Delete if not
applicable.

(2) If Deponent did
not serve demand
delete 'I' and insert
name and address of
person who effected
service, as applicable.
Before or after
‡ 1600 hours
Monday to
Friday, before or
after 1200 hours
Saturday.

(3) Insert date.

(4) Insert exact
address of service.

(5) Delete words in
[ ] if no
acknowledgement of
service has been
received.

(6) Give particulars of
the way in which the
Debtor acknowledged
service of the Demand.
(Acknowledgement
must be in writing).

(7) State full
address.

IN THE*

In Bankruptcy

Re

Date of Statutory Demand

I (¹)

† [a person acting on behalf of] [the Creditor]
MAKE OATH AND SAY AS FOLLOWS:-

1.   (²) [I] [

                                             ]

did on (³) the   day of
before [after]   ‡hours (⁴) at

personally serve the above-named Debtor with the Demand
dated (³) the   day of

(⁵) [2.   That on (³) the   day of
the Debtor acknowledged service of the Demand by (⁶)

                                             ]

3.   A copy of the Demand marked "A" (⁵) [and the acknowledgement of
service marked "B"] is (⁵) [are] exhibited hereto.

SWORN at (⁷)

the   day of
Before me,

                                }

Solicitor/A Commissioner for Oaths

day of

Filed the

Creditors bankruptcy petition (Insolvency - Bankruptcy 6.7)

FORM 6.7

In the[†]

No. of

Rule 6.6 Creditor's Bankruptcy Petition on Failure to Comply with a Statutory Demand for a Liquidated Sum Payable Immediately

IN BANKRUPTCY

† Enter "High Court of Justice" or "_____County Court" as the case may be.

‡ Insert full name of Debtor (if known)

RE ‡

(a) Insert full name(s) and address(es) of petitioner(s)

I/We[(a)]

(b) Insert full name, place of residence and occupation (if any) of debtor

petition the court that a bankruptcy order may be made against [(b)]

(c) Insert in full any other name(s) by which the debtor is or has been known

[also known as [(c)]

(d) Insert trading name (adding "with another or others", if this is so), business address and nature of business

[and carrying on business as [(d)]

]

(e) Insert any other address or addresses at which the debtor has resided at or after the time the petition debt was incurred

[and lately residing at [(e)]

]

(f) Give the same details as specified in note (d) above for any other businesses which have been carried on at or after the time the petition debt was incurred

[and lately carrying on business as [(f)]

]

and say as follows:-

1. The debtor has for the greater part of six months immediately preceding the

(g) Delete as applicable

presentation of this petition [(g)] [resided at] [carried on business at]

(h) Or as the case may be following the terms of Rule 6.9

within the district of this court[(h)]

(j) Please give the amount of debt(s), what they relate to and when they were incurred. Please show separately the amount or rate of any interest or other charge not previously notified to the debtor and the reasons why you are claiming it

2. The debtor is justly and truly indebted to me[us] in the aggregate sum of £[(j)]

3. The above-mentioned debt is for a liquidated sum payable immediately and the debtor appears to be unable to pay it.

TSO 12 Insolvency – Bankruptcy 6.7: 1 of 2

You need this book first

(k) Insert date of service of a statutory demand

4. On (k)

a statutory demand was served upon the debtor by

(l) State manner of service of demand

(l)

in respect of the above-mentioned debt. To the best of my knowledge and belief the demand has neither been complied with nor set aside in accordance with the Rules and no application to set it aside is outstanding

(m) If 3 weeks have not elapsed since service of statutory demand give reasons for earlier presentation of petition

(m)

5. I/We do not, nor does any person on my/our behalf, hold any security on the debtor's estate, or any part thereof, for the payment of the above-mentioned sum OR

(n) Delete as applicable

I/We hold security for the payment of (n) [part of] of the above-mentioned sum I/We will give up such security for the benefit of all the creditors in the event of a bankruptcy order being made OR

I/We hold security for the payment of part of the above-mentioned sum and I/we estimate the value of such security to be £

This petition is not made in respect of the secured part of my/our debt

---

Endorsement

This petition having been presented to the court on

it is ordered that the petition shall be heard as follows:-

Date

Time   hours

Place

(p) Insert name of debtor

and you, the above-named (p)   , are to take

notice that if you intend to oppose the petition you must not later than 7 days before the day fixed for the hearing:

  (i)   file in court a notice (in Form 6.19) specifying the grounds on which you object to the making of a bankruptcy order; and

  (ii) send a copy of the notice to the petitioner or his solicitor

(q) Only to be completed where the petitioning creditor is represented by a solicitor

The solicitor to the petitioning creditor is:- (q)

Name

Address

Telephone Number

Reference

Affidavit of truth of statements in bankruptcy petition (Insolvency - Bankruptcy 6.13)

Filed on behalf of:
Name of Deponent:
No. of Affidavit:
Exhibit Initials and No.:
Date Affidavit Sworn:

Form 6.13
Affidavit of Truth of Statements in Bankruptcy Petition. (Rule 6.12).

No. of

IN THE*

*Enter "High Court of Justice" *or* "_______ County Court" as the case may be.

In Bankruptcy

Re

(1) Insert name, address, description (occupation) of person making Oath.

I (1)

MAKE OATH AND SAY AS FOLLOWS:-

[1. I am the Petitioner. The statements in the Petition now produced and shown to me marked "A" are true to the best of my knowledge, information and belief.

2. (2)

]

(2) If Petition is based upon a statutory demand, and more than 4 months have elapsed between service of the demand and presentation of the Petition, give reason(s) for delay and explanation of circumstances which have contributed to the late presentation of the Petition.

OR

[1. I am (3) the of the Petitioner.

OR

2. I am duly authorised by the Petitioner to make this Affidavit on (4) [its] [his] behalf.

(3) State the capacity eg. director, company secretary, or similar company officer, solicitor etc.

(4) Delete as applicable.

3. I have been concerned in the matters giving rise to the presentation of the Petition and I have the requisite knowledge of the matters referred to in the Petition because (5)

(5) State means of knowledge of matters sworn to in the affidavit.

4. The statements in the Petition now produced and shown to me marked "A" are true to the best of my knowledge, information and belief.

5. (2)

]

(6) State full address.

SWORN at (6)

the day of

Before me,

Solicitor/A Commissioner for Oaths

Filed the day of

TSO 13 Insolvency – Bankruptcy 6.13: 1 of 1

You need this book first

Affidavit of personal service of bankruptcy petition (Insolvency - Bankruptcy 6.17)

Form 6.17

Affidavit of
Personal Service
of Bankruptcy
Petition
(Rule 6.15)

*Enter High Court of
Justice or "_____
County Court" as the
case may be.

(1) Insert name of
debtor as in title of
Petition.

(2) Insert date.

(3) Insert full name,
address, description
(occupation) of
person making
oath.

(4) Insert full name
and address.

(5) Delete as
applicable.

† Delete whichever
is inapplicable
(Before/after 1600
hours Monday to
Friday; before/after
1200 hours
Saturday).

(6) Insert name of
Debtor as in title.

(7) State exact place
of service.

(8) Sealed copy
must be marked
as an exhibit.

(9) State full
address.

Filed on behalf of:
Name of Deponent:
No. of Affidavit:
Exhibit Initials and No.:
Date Affidavit Sworn:

IN THE*   **No.**   of

In Bankruptcy

Re (¹)

IN THE MATTER OF a Bankruptcy Petition filed
on (²) the   day of
I (³)

and for the purpose of service instructed by (⁴)

(5) [Solicitor(s) for] the Petitioning Creditor

MAKE OATH AND SAY AS FOLLOWS:-

1. That I did on (²)   day the   day of
before [after]   †hours serve the
above-named Debtor with a copy of the above-mentioned Petition,
duly sealed with the seal of the court by delivering the same
personally to the said (⁶)

at (⁷)

2.   A sealed copy of the said Petition is now produced and shown to
me makred "A" (⁸).

SWORN at (⁹)

⎫
⎬
⎭

the   day of
Before me,

A Solicitor/A Commissioner for Oaths,

**Note:- This affidavit and exhibit should be filed in court immediately after
service (Rule 6.15.(2)).**

TSO 14 Insolvency – Bankruptcy 6.17: 1 of 1

Statutory demand (Insolvency - Company 4.1)

Statutory Demand
under section 123(1)(a)
or 222(1)(a) of the
Insolvency Act 1986 No.
4.1* (Rule 4.5)

WARNING

- This is an **important** document. This demand must be dealt with **within 21 days** after its service upon the company or a winding-up order could be made in respect of the company.

- Please read the demand and notes carefully.

DEMAND

To

Address

This demand is served on you by the Creditor:

Name
Address

The Creditor claims that the Company owes the sum of £   , full particulars of which are set out on page 2,

NOTES FOR CREDITOR

1. If the Creditor is entitled to the debt by way of assignment, details of the original Creditor and any intermediary assignees should be given in part B on page 3.

2. If the amount of debt includes interest not previously notified to the Company as included in its liability, details should be given, including the grounds upon which interest is charged. The amount of interest must be shown separately.

3. Any other charge accruing due from time to time may be claimed. The amount or rate of the charge must be identified and the grounds on which it is claimed must be stated.

4. In either case the amount claimed must be limited to that which has accrued due at the date of the demand.

5. If signatory of the demand is a solicitor or other agent of the Creditor, the name of his/her firm should be given.

The Creditor demands that the Company do pay the above debt or secure or compound for it to the Creditor's satisfaction.

Signature of individual

Name
(BLOCK LETTERS)

Dated

* Position with or relationship to Creditor

*I am authorised to make this demand on the Creditor's behalf.

Address

Tel. No.   Ref No.

* Delete if signed by the Creditor himself.

N.B. The person making this Demand must complete the whole of this page, page 2 and parts A and B (as applicable) on page 3.

[P.T.O

TSO 15 Insolvency – Company 4.1: 1 of 4

You need this book first

Particulars of Debt (These particulars must include **(a)** when the debt was incurred, **(b)** the consideration for the debt (or if there is no consideration the way in which it arose) and **(c)** the amount due as at the date of this demand).

NOTES FOR CREDITOR

1. If the Creditor is entitled to the debt by way of assignment, details of the original Creditor and any intermediary assignees should be given in part B on page 3.

2. If the amount of debt includes interest not previously notified to the Company as included in its liability, details should be given, including the grounds upon which interest is charged. The amount of interest must be shown separately.

3. Any other charge accruing due from time to time may be claimed. The amount or rate of the charge must be identified and the grounds on which it is claimed must be stated.

4. In either case the amount claimed must be limited to that which has accrued due at the date of the demand.

5. If signatory of the demand is a solicitor or other agent of the Creditor, the name of his/her firm should be given.

NOTE
If space is insufficient continue on reverse of page 3 and clearly indicate on this page that you are doing so.

TSO 15 Insolvency – Company 4.1: 2 of 4

Part A

The individual or individuals to whom any communication regarding this demand may be addressed is/are:

Name
(BLOCK LETTERS)

Address

Postcode

Telephone Number

Reference

Part B

For completion if the Creditor is entitled to the debt by way of assignment.

	Name	Date(s) of Assignment
Original Creditor		
Assignees		

How to comply with a Statutory Demand

If the Company wishes to avoid a winding-up Petition being presented it must pay the debt shown on page 1, particulars of which are set out on page 2 of this notice, within the period of **21 days** after its service upon the Company. Alternatively, the Company can attempt to come to a settlement with the Creditor. To do this the Company should:

• Inform the individual (or one of the individuals) named in Part A immediately that it is willing and able to offer security for the debt to the Creditor's satisfaction; *or*

• inform the individual (or one of the individuals) named in Part A immediately that it is willing and able to compound for the debt to the Creditor's satisfaction.

If the Company disputes the demand in whole or in part it should:

• contact the individual (or one of the individuals) named in Part A above immediately.

> **Remember!** **The Company has only 21 days after the date of service on it of this document before the Creditor may present a winding-up Petition.**

TSO 15 Insolvency – Company 4.1: 3 of 4

You need this book first

Winding-up petition (Insolvency - company 4.2)

Winding-up
Petition
No. 4.2 (Rule 4.7)

IN THE   **No.**   **of**

(1) Insert name of Company.

IN THE MATTER of (¹)

AND

IN THE MATTER of the Insolvency Act 1986

(2) Insert title of Court.

To (²)

(3) Insert full name(s) and address(es) of Petitioner(s).

The Petition of (³)

(4) Insert date of incorporation.

1.   Limited (¹)
(hereinafter called "the Company") was incorporated on (⁴)
under the Companies Act 19   .

(5) Insert address of registered office.

2.   The registered office of the Company is at (⁵)

3.   The nominal capital of the Company is £   divided into
          shares of £   each. The amount of the capital paid up or
credited as paid up is £

4.   The principal objects for which the Company was established are as follows:-

and other objects stated in the Memorandum of Association of the Company.

(6) Set out the grounds on which a Winding-up Order is sought.

5.   (⁶)

[P.T.O

TSO 16 Insolvency – Company 4.2: 1 of 4

159

You need this book first

Note:- This margin is reserved for binding and must not be written across.

160

6. In the circumstances it is just and equitable that the Company should be wound up.

Your Petitioner therefore prays as follows:-

(1) That (¹)

Limited, may be wound up by the Court under the provisions of the Insolvency Act 1986 or

(2) That such other Order may be made as the Court thinks fit.

(⁷) If the Company is Petitioner delete note and add the words "It is not intended to serve this Petition upon any person". Add the full name and address of any other person on whom it is intended to serve the Petition.

Note:- (¹) It is intended to serve this Petition on the Company.

You need this book first

Endorsement

This Petition having been presented to the court

(a) Delete as applicable.

(b) Insert name and address of Court.

(c) Insert name and address of District Registry.

on: will be heard at (a) [Royal Courts of Justice, Strand, London WC2A 2LL] [(b)   County Court]

[(c)   District Registry   ]

on:

Date

Time   hours
  (or as soon thereafter as the Petition can be heard)

The solicitor to the Petitioner is:-

Name

Address

Telephone No.

Reference

(a) [Whose London Agents are:-

Name

Address

Telephone No.

Reference   ]

Affidavit verifying winding up petition (Insolvency - Company 4.3)

No.   of

IN THE

Sworn
Filed

IN THE MATTER of

AND

IN THE MATTER of the Insolvency Act 1986.

AFFIDAVIT
Verifying Petition

Filed on behalf of the Petitioner.

Petitioner's Solicitor

TSO 17 Insolvency – Company 4.3; 1 of 2

You need this book first

Affidavit Verifying
Winding-Up
Petition
No. 4.3 (Rules 4.7
and 4.12)

Filed on behalf of the Petitioner.
Deponent :
No. of Affidavit :
Exhibit Initials and No. :
Date Affidavit Sworn :

IN THE   No.   of

IN THE MATTER OF

AND

IN THE MATTER of the Insolvency Act 1986

(1) Insert name and address of person making oath.

I, (¹)

MAKE OATH AND SAY AS FOLLOWS:-

(2) Delete if Affidavit not made by Petitioner in person.

(3) Delete as applicable.

1.(²)   I am the Petitioner. The statements in the Petition now produced and shown to me marked "A" are (³) [true] [true to the best of my knowledge, information and belief].

(4) Delete if Affidavit is made by Petitioner in person.

(5) State capacity eg. director, secretary, solicitor etc.

1.(⁴)   I am (⁵)
of the Petitioner.

2.(⁴)   I am duly authorised by the Petitioner to make this Affidavit on (³) [its] [his] behalf.

3.(⁴)   I have been concerned in the matters giving rise to the Petition and have the requisite knowledge of the matters referred to in the Petition because (⁶)

(6) State means of knowledge of matters sworn to in Affidavit.

4.(⁴)   The statements in the Petition now produced and shown to me marked "A" are (³) [true] [true to the best of my knowledge, information and belief].

SWORN at   ⎫
                                   ⎬
this   day of   ⎭

Before me,

A Solicitor

TSO 17 Insolvency – Company 4.3: 2 of 2

Affidavit of service of winding-up petition at registered office (Insolvency - Company 4.4)

No.   of

IN THE

Sworn

Filed

IN THE MATTER of   Limited

and

IN THE MATTER of the Insolvency Act 1986.

Affidavit

OF SERVICE OF PETITION

Filed on behalf of the Petitioner.

TSO 18 Insolvency – Company 4.4: 1 of 2

Affidavit of
Service of Winding-Up
Petition at
Registered Office
No. 4.4 (Rule 4.9)

Note: If the Petition
was served on an
officer or an
employee of the
company use **Part A**
of this form. If it was served
on a person authorised to
accept service on behalf of
the company use
Part B. If it was
served by depositing
it at the registered
office use **Part C.**

Filed on behalf of the Petitioner.

Deponent :

No. of Affidavit :

Exhibit Initials and No. :

Date Affidavit Sworn :

IN THE HIGH COURT OF JUSTICE
Chancery Division
Companies Court

No. of

IN THE MATTER OF

AND

IN THE MATTER of the Insolvency Act 1986

(1) Insert name,
address and
description of person
making oath.

I (¹)

MAKE OATH AND SAY AS FOLLOWS:-

(2) Insert date.

Part A.
That I did on (²) serve the above-named Company with a sealed copy of
the Petition now produced and shown to me marked "A" by handing the same to
(³) [who acknowledged himself to be]
[who is to the best of my knowledge, information and belief (³)] [a director] [an officer]
[an employee] of the Company at (⁴)

(3) Delete as
applicable.

(4) Insert address of
registered office.

the registered office of the said company.
OR
Part B.
That I did on (²) serve the above-named Company with a sealed copy of
the Petition now produced and shown to me marked "A" by handing the same to
who acknowledged to me that he was
authorised to accept service of documents on behalf of the Company at (⁴)

the registered office of the said company.
OR
Part C.
That I did on (²) having failed to find any officer, employee or other
person authorised to accept service of documents on behalf of the Company, deposit a
sealed copy of the Petition now produced and shown to me marked "A" at (⁴)

(5) Insert where the Petition
was left in
such a way that it was likely
to come to the attention of
a person attending the
registered office e.g. on a
desk, through the letter
box, affixed to the above,
etc.

the registered office of the said company by leaving it (⁵)

Sworn at

this day of

Before me,

A Solicitor

TSO 18 Insolvency – Company 4.4: 2 of 2

166

Affidavit of service winding-up petition other than at registered office or on an oversea company (Insolvency - Company 4.5)

Form 4.5

Rule 4.9

Note: If the petition was served on an officer or on an employee of the company use Part A of this form. If it was served on a person authorised to accept service on behalf of the company use Part B. If the petition was served on an oversea company use Part C only.

(a) Insert name, address and description of person making oath.

(b) State reason why petition has been served at an address other than a registered office

(c) Insert date

(d) Delete as applicable

(e) Insert address at which service effected

(f) Insert class of postage

(g) Insert name

AFFIDAVIT OF SERVICE OF WINDING-UP PETITION OTHER THAN AT REGISTERED OFFICE OR ON AN OVERSEA COMPANY

(TITLE)

I (a)

make oath and say as follows

1. (b)

Part A

2. That I did on (c)   serve the above-named company with a sealed copy of the petition now produced and shown to me marked "A" by handing the same to   (d) [who acknowledged himself to be] [who is to the best of my knowledge, information and belief] (d) [a director] [an officer] [an employee] of the company at (e)

(d) [the company's last known principal place of business in England and Wales] [a place where the company carried on business in England and Wales]

or
Part B

2. That I did on (c)   serve, the above-named company with a sealed copy of the petition now produced and shown to me marked "A" by handing the same to   who acknowledged to me that he was authorised to accept service of documents on behalf of the company at (e)

(d) [the company's last known principal place of business in England and Wales] [a place where the company carried on business in England and Wales].

or
Part C

That I did on (c)   serve the above-named company with a sealed copy of the petition now produced and shown to me marked "A" by (d) [leaving it] [sending it by (f)   post] to (e)

(d) [the address of (g)

whose name has been delivered to the Registrar of Companies as a person authorised to accept on the said company's behalf service of process and any notices required to be served on it] [a place of business established by the said company in Great Britain].

Sworn at

TSO 19 Insolvency – Company 4.5: 1 of 1

You need this book first

Application for a fee exemption or remission (EX160)

Application for a Fee Exemption or Remission	**For the Court's use only.**	
	In the	County Court
	Reference Number	
	Evidence for automatic exemption? Yes ☐ No ☐ *Benefits at Note 4C, or green form if family case*	
	Remission granted? Yes ☐ No ☐	
	Court fee	
	Amount exempted or remitted	
	Signed	
	Date	
	Grade	

1. About the case.

a Name of Plaintiff or Petitioner. — *in BLOCK LETTERS*

b Name of Defendant or Respondent. — *in BLOCK LETTERS*

c The **Case Number**, if you know it.

d The title of the form which you would like the Court to issue:
See Note 4A.

2. About you.

a Surname or family name. — *in BLOCK LETTERS*

b Other names. — *in BLOCK LETTERS*

c Title. — Mr ☐ Mrs ☐ Miss ☐ Ms ☐

d Address.

e Marital status. — Married ☐ Single ☐ Other ☐

f Are you receiving legal advice under the Green Form Scheme, in a Family case?
If you answer Yes, please give your solicitor's name, reference, address and daytime telephone number.
See Note 4e.

No ☐ Go to question 2g.

Yes ☐ Put your solicitor's details in the boxes below. Then go to part 9.

Solicitor's Name:	Ref.
Address	

g Are you receiving:
Family Credit
or Income Support
or Income-based Job-Seekers Allowance
or Disability Working Allowance?

Telephone number (daytime)

No ☐ Go to part 3. *See Note 4o.*

Yes ☐ Read note 4c. Then go to Part 9 and sign and date the Declaration.

TSO 20 EX160: 1 of 2

168

3. Dependants (people whom you look after financially).

The number of children aged:

under 11		11–15		16–17		18	

Other dependants.
Give details.

4. Employment.

Are you employed?   No [ ]   Yes [ ]   Type of employment

Are you self-employed?   No [ ]   Yes [ ]   Type of employment

Are you unemployed?   No [ ]   Yes [ ]   How long have you been unemployed?

Are you a pensioner?   No [ ]   Yes [ ]

5. Your property.

Do you live:
✓ one box

in your own property? [ ]   in lodgings? [ ]   in rented property? [ ]

in property which you own jointly with someone else? [ ]

in other property? [ ]   Please explain
(for instance, with your parents)

6. Your savings.

Give an amount for each type of savings. If you do not have one of the types shown, put NIL.

Bank account (Current)	£	Premium Bonds	£
Bank account (Deposit)	£	Stock and Shares (or both)	£
Building Society Accounts (1)	£	National Saving Investments	£
(2)	£	Other Savings which are:	
			£

7. Your usual monthly income.

Give an amount for each type of income. If you do not have one of the types of income shown, put NIL. Add up the amounts and put the sum in the Total income each month box.

Your usual take home pay	£	Child Benefit	£
Your partner's usual take home pay (*if applicable*)	£	Other benefit(s) which are:	£
Income from other people who live with you	£		£
Your pension(s) *(put the total)*	£	**Total income each month**	£

8. Your usual monthly expenses.

Give an amount for each type of expense. If you do not have one of the expenses, put NIL. Add up the amounts and put the sum in the Total expenses each month box.

Rent or Mortgage	£	Child care	£
Council Tax (*give the amount you actually pay*)	£	Travelling Expenses	£
		Food and household essentials	£
Water and Sewerage charges	£	Court fines	£
Maintenance and Child Support	£	Clothing	£
Electricity	£	Other expenses which are:	
Gas, coal and oil	£		£
Telephone	£		£
TV rent and licence	£	**Total expenses each month**	£

9. Declaration.

I declare that the information which I have given is true to the best of my knowledge and belief. I understand that I may be asked to provide documents as evidence to support my statements and that my application will not proceed if I do not provide the evidence. I also understand that my application will be refused if I have not disclosed any relevant facts in this form.

Signed _____   Date _____

TSO 20   EX160: 2 of 2

You need this book first

Useful contacts

The Central Index (of company winding-up petitions)

To check to see if someone else has already filed a winding-up petition, search the Central Index which is maintained by

The Companies Court
Room TM 209
Royal Courts of Justice
Thomas More Building
The Strand
London WC2A 2LL
Tel: 020 7936 7328

Companies House

Companies House has seven offices in England, Wales and Scotland. Its headquarters are in Cardiff:

Companies House
Crown Way
Cardiff CF-143UZ
Tel: 029 2038 8588
General enquiries: 0870 3333636

Companies House maintains a register of disqualified directors. Ring the general enquiries number above and give them the person's surname and initial. They can usually check over the telephone. This is a free service. They will also provide full details (addresses, occupations, dates of appointment, etc) of existing directors for £4 per company if you want the results posted, £5 if you want them faxed. Alternatively, you can access information on their website:

http://www.companies.house.gov.uk

Data Protection Registrar

Wycliffe House
Water Lane
Wilmslow
Cheshire SK9 5AF
Information line: 01625 545745
To register: 01625 545740
Switchboard: 01625 545700
Fax: 01625 524510

Email: data@wycliffe.demon.co.uk
Website: http//www.dataprotection.gov.uk

HM Land Registry

HM Land Registry
32 Lincoln's Inns Fields
London WC2A 3PH
Tel: 0207 917 8888

The Individual Insolvency Register

The Individual Insolvency Register keeps details of bankruptcy and individual voluntary arrangements.

- *Go in person* to any Official Receiver's office (listed in your local telephone directory), fill in a form and receive a printout of the information;

- *Write to*
  The Insolvency Service
  5th Floor
  West Wing
  45 – 46 Stephenson Street
  Birmingham D24UP

- *Telephone* the Insolvency Service helpline on 0207 637 1110 and they will tell you over the phone whether an individual is bankrupt (or is subject to bankruptcy proceedings) or has entered into an IVA. There is no charge. The same number will also tell you whether a company has gone into compulsory liquidation or is subject to liquidation proceedings, or has entered into a company voluntary arrangement (CVA). Again, there is no charge.

Insolvency in London

For individuals contact:

Bankruptcy Court
Royal Courts of Justice
Thomas More Building
The Strand
London WC2A 2LL
Tel: 0207 936 6448
Fax: 0207 936 6958

For companies contact:

Companies Court
Royal Courts of justice
Thomas More Building
The Strand
London WC2A 2LL
Tel: 0207 936 6294
Fax: 0207 936 6928

London Gazette

To advertise your winding-up petition send it to:

London Gazette
PO Box 7293
London SE1 5ZH
Tel: 0207 394 4580

Remember to include your cheque for £26.81 (inclusive of VAT) payable to the *London Gazette.* Give at least two days' notice of the date you wish the advertisement to appear.

Lord Chancellor's Department

The Court Service is an executive agency of the Lord Chancellor's Department which provides administrative support to the High Court and County Courts.

The Court Service
Southside
105 Victoria Street
London SW1E 6QT
Tel: 0207 210 2266
Website: http://www.courtservice.gov.uk

Register of County Court Judgments

Registry Trust Limited
173/175 Cleveland Street
London W1P 5PE
Tel: 0207 380 0133

For £4.50 a name (make out the cheque to Registry Trust Limited) you can get a printout of any judgments against that name.

Index

Administration of Justice Act (1970) 17
affidavits 7, 89, 150, 165–6, 167
   bankruptcy 80–1, 82, 153, 154
   liquidation 88
   of service 69, 115–16
   winding-up petition 163–4
attachment of earnings 7, 48, 57–8
   court procedure 59–62
   order 20
   as worthwhile 58
Attachment of Earnings Index 59

bailiff 7, 30, 51, 53–4, 55, 56–7, 75
bankruptcy 8, 19
   considerations 73–5
   cost 30–1
   court procedure 76–85
   creditors 29
   described 71–3
   threat 28–9, 73, 76

Central Index 88, 171
Centralised Attachment of Earnings Payments System
   (CAPS) 60, 62
certificate of compliance (liquidation) 127
Certificate that the Debt is Still Due and Owing 83–4
charging order 8, 31, 48, 66

considerations 66–7
court procedure 67–70
do it yourself 67
ex parte 10, 69
nisi 66, 69, 110–11, 112–14
claim form *see* Form N1 (claim form)
claimant 8, 35, 42
Companies House 22, 52, 87, 171
conduct money 9, 51
consolidated orders 59, 62
contract
claiming interest under 40–2
complaints procedure 28
considerations 23
terms 19, 20
costs
attachment of earnings 59
bank fees 65
bankruptcy 30, 73, 75, 81, 82–3
charging order 68
court fees 16, 30, 38, 54, 61, 64, 68,
73, 75, 81, 82, 88
enforcement 49
garnishee order 64, 65
Land Registry 68
solicitors 38
warrant of execution 54, 55
winding-up advertisement 90
counterclaim 9
County Court 30–1
choosing 32–4
fees 16, 38, 54, 61, 64, 68,

75, 81, 82, 88
Judgments Register 14
service 43–4
County Courts Act (1994) 41
credit reference agency 22–3
creditors 29, 74, 84
bankruptcy petition 117–19
secured 14
customer
doubtful 21–3
final warning 26
first reminder 24
invoice 24
ongoing enquiries 26
ring the debtor 24, 26
stiff letter 24
CVA (company voluntary arrangement) 9

Data Protection Registrar 172
debt collection
agency 16
claim for time 20
solicitor 16–17
debt recovery
court action 32–46
enforcement 47–91
initial phase 24–31
debtor
bankruptcy options 79–80
changes jobs 62
contacting 24–6

earnings 57–61
file acknowledgment of service 45
harassment 17
options 44–5
oral examination 48–51
removal of goods 53
suspension of orders 55–6, 60–1
unemployed 61
default judgment 9, 45, 46
defendant 9, 35–6, 37

enforcement 10, 47
attachment of earnings 57–62
bankruptcy 71–85
charging order 66–71
garnishee order 62–5
liquidation 85–91
oral examination 48–52
points to consider 47–8
warrant of execution 53–7
ex parte 10, 69

fast track 10
Form 4.1 (statutory demand – insolvency – company)
    87, 88, 155–8
Form 4.2 (winding-up petition) 88, 120–4, 159–62
Form 4.3 (affidavit verifying winding-up petition) 89,
    163–4
Form 4.4 (affidavit of service of winding-up petition at
    registered office) 89, 165–6

Form 4.5 (affidavit of service of winding–up petition other than at registered office) 89, 167

Form 6.1; 6.2 (statutory demand – insolvency – bankruptcy) 76–8, 142–5, 146–9

Form 6.11 (affidavit of personal service of statutory demand) 79, 81, 150

Form 6.13 (affidavit of truth of statements in bankruptcy petition) 80–1, 82, 153

Form 6.17 (affidavit of personal service of bankruptcy petition) 82, 154

Form 6.7 (creditors bankruptcy petition) 80, 81, 117–19, 151–2

Form 96 (Land Registry) 67

Form 109 (Land Registry) 68

Form CT2 (Land Registry) 70

Form EX160 (Application for a fee exemption or remission) 168–9

Form N1 (claim form) 4, 8
    amount claimed 37, 38
    claim number 34
    claimant details 35
    claimant's solicitor's address 42
    court fee 38, 42–3
    defendant (debtor) details 35–6, 37
    details of claim 37
    filling in 34–42
    interest 39–42
    issue date 38
    keep a copy 43
    name of court 34
    particulars of claim 39–42, 98–9

samples 98–9, 130–3
solicitor's costs 38
statement of truth 42
take/post 42–3
value 37
Form N56 (Reinstatement of Attachment of Earnings) 61
Form N215 (certificate of service) 43, 134–5
Form N244 (Request for court reconsideration) 61
Form N316 (Request for Oral Examination) 49, 136
Form N323 (Request for Warrant of Execution) 54, 137
Form N337 (Request for Attachment of Earnings) 59, 139
Form N349 (Affidavit in support of Application for Garnishee Order Absolute) 65, 141
Form N445 (Request for Reissue of Warrant) 55, 138
Form N446 (Request for Reissue of Enforcement or Oral Examination) 61, 62, 140
forms, filling in 4–5

garnishee order 10, 31, 48, 62-4
    court procedure 64–5
goods
    disputed ownership 56–7
    holding on to 23
    jointly owned 57
    keeping and selling 18
    removal 53, 57
    taking back 18

High Court 11, 31
    bankruptcy 77–8, 81, 82–3
    London Insolvency District 77–8
HM Land Registry 67–8, 70, 172
home court 32, 34, 49, 52, 97

Individual Insolvency Register 21–2, 80, 173
individual voluntary arrangement (IVA) 11, 79, 80
Insolvency Service helpline 22
instalment order 11
interest
    claiming 20, 39–42
    contractual claim 40–2
    daily rate 41–2
    judgment debt 20
    statutory rights 40, 41

judgment 11
judgment debt 11, 75
    claiming interest 20
    pursuing enforcement 20

Late Payment of Commercial Debts (Interest) Act
    (1998) 40, 41
lawspeak 5–6
letter of claim 11–12, 95
letters
    first reminder 93
    red warning (letter of claim) 95

summing up debtor's proposals for payment 96
transfer to home court 97
yellow warning 94
liquidation 12, 85–6
certificate of compliance 127
cost 30–1
creditors 29
procedure 88–91
statutory demand stage 87
threat 28–9
litigant 12
litigation 12
London Gazette 90, 125, 174–5
London Insolvency District 77–8, 86
Lord Chancellor's Department 175

multi-track 12

nisi 13
*Notice of Issue (Specified Amount) and Request for
Judgment* 43

Official Receiver 13, 73, 85
on-the-spot notes 26
oral examination 13, 48–9
debtor does not show 51
hearing 49–51
limited company/firm 52
procedure 49

payment
   can pay, won't pay 27–8
   can't pay 27
   cleared funds 23
   interim 19
   non-payment as criminal offence 17
   proposals 96
   withholding goods 18
personal service 13, 44, 51, 75, 78–9, 89
petition 14
preferential debts 14, 74

Register of County Court Judgments 14, 21, 175
Register of Disqualified Directors 22–3
Registry Trust Limited 21
response time 44

service 14, 43
small claims track 15
Small Print, The 28
solicitor 16–17, 38, 42
Statement of Means 50, 100–9
statutory demand 15, 75–6
   insolvency – company 87, 88, 155–8
   procedure 76–80
sueing 19
summary judgment 15

track 15

walking possession agreements 56
warrant of execution 15, 48, 53–4, 75
   court procedure 54–7
   disputed ownership 56–7
   walking possession agreements 56
winding-up petition 88, 120–4, 159–62, 163–4,
     165–6
   advertisement 90, 125–6

Printed in the United Kingdom by The Stationery Office Ltd., London
TJ5199   C20   10/01   652056   19585